Improve Your English

Learn it-Yourself Books are specially designed to enable the readers to learn useful skills and techniques, and obtain sound, authoritative information of value in their professional, family and personal lives.

The subjects of these books have been selected on the criteria of their utility for a large number of readers. The books are comprehensive, and in some cases, are designed as work-books to serve the readers as self-learning guides.

Principal D.D. Vaid, the author of this book is a reputed educationist from Punjab, who in his long 40 years of experience — as a professor of English and later as a principal of a degree college — has taught English to thousands of students. He has made an extensive study of the type of errors usually committed by students as well as scholars in speaking and writing English.

"Makes the task very easy for the beginners as well as others who are keen to learn how to write and speak chaste, idiomatic and flawless English in their day-to-day work and life."

Pioneer

"D.D. Vaid has long experience in teaching English, first as a professor of English and later as Head of the English Department, Punjab University. This book will surely help the students, writers and others to write and speak English correctly."

Nagpur Times

IMPROVE YOUR ENGLISH

D.D. Vaid, M.A., B.Sc. (Hons)
Former Principal, Degree College, Dabwali
Ex-Head, English Department, Punjab University

Orient Paperbacks
DELHI | MUMBAI | HYDERABAD

www.orientpaperbacks.com

ISBN : 978-81-222-0040-9

1st Published 1977
16th Printing 2016

Improve Your English

Cover design by Vision Studio

Published by
Orient Paperbacks
(A division of Vision Books Pvt. Ltd.)
5A/8 Ansari Road, New Delhi-110 002

Printed at Artxel, Noida

CONTENTS

INTRODUCTION

ENGLISH LANGUAGE, spoken as well as written, continues to dominate all over the world. In every field of activity, whether social, cultural, official or political, it has become almost a part of the everyday life of an individual. So, the necessity of cultivating the habit of speaking and writing this language correctly is of prime importance for both a layman and a sophisticated worker, whoever strives at making some progress in life. It is all the more imperative for a student in school or college as well as a scholar or teacher for obvious reasons.

I have endeavoured to present in this small volume all that is essential in English grammar in a manner that is easy to learn and grasp, and thus enable every one to write English free from errors, so commonly made in our everyday utterances and writings.

In doing so, my long exprience as a teacher of English in first grade degree colleges connected with the Punjab University—first as a lecturer and later, as Head of the Department of English, and as Principal—has helped me a good deal or speak in it.

By carefully going through the book, the reader will become aware that most of the errors are committed owing to the lack of knowledge of the various rules of grammar, pertaining to the correct usage of the different parts of speech such as the Preposition, Noun, Article, etc., in a sentence. He will further realise how to understand the beauty of the syntax, and, what words to use or omit to avoid the common mistakes—which are called 'Indianisms'. These arise, most often, from a habit of translating literally the syntax of our Indian languages into English, though these differ very much. There are certain subtleties and peculiarities in the English syntax and grammar which have to be learnt through a careful study.

Learning the rules of grammar of any language, especially that of English is a very dull and tedious job. A student generally shirks this part of the language, but to attain a certain proficiency in English he cannot avoid doing so wholly. To make this task easy for a reader, especially a student, I have listed up the incorrect and the correct sentences opposite each other and then the error in the sentence is made clear by referring to the relevant rule of grammar which cover all such similar cases.

To make the book instructive I have added other chapters also on 'spellings' or the words that are confused in their usage or phrases which get mixed up frequently when they are spoken or written in a sentence.

I have added at the end, a chapter on everyday proverbs and quotations from eminent authors, to be used by students in their essays or speeches and this added senterest will surely make the book all the more attractive.

I am confident that a proper study of the various chapters will surely benefit the reader and help him to write chaste and flawless English.

I shall be grateful for any suggestion to improve this book in the later editions, from the readers.

616-L, Model Town
Ludhiana

D.D. Vaid
Prof. of English

NOUNS

ERRORS COMMITTED IN THE USE OF NOUNS

Incorrect	*Correct*
The *sceneries* of Kashmir are very fine.	The *scenery* of Kashmir is very fine.
Where have you placed my *furnitures*?	Where have you placed my *furniture*?
Several type of *machineries* were installed in that factory.	Several type of *machinery* was installed in that factory.
Have you received any *informations*?	Have you received any *information*?
The *cavalries* of the British attacked Germans.	The *cavalry* of the British attacked Germans.
The price of *cattles* has gone up.	The price of *cattle* has gone up.
He studies several type of *poetries*.	He studies several type of *poetry*.
He is guilty of so *many mischiefs*.	He is guilty of so *much mischief*.
Mohan purchased several type of *fuels*.	Mohan purchased several type of *fuel*.
There are so many *filths* all around the place.	There is so much *filth* all around the place.

The *infantries* of Germans fell back.	The *infantry* of Germans fell back.
Your *perfumeries* seem to be very costly.	Your *perfumery* seems to be very costly.
Have the *corns* been cut?	Has the *corn* been cut?
He took several type of *foods.*	He took several type of *food.*
Seven *clergys* were seen in that church	Seven *clergy* were seen in that church.
Many *peoples* attended the function.	Many *people* attended the function.
I am sick of your *behaviours.*	I am sick of your *behaviour.*
Mohan has different type of *poultries* in his farm.	Mohan has different type of *poultry* in his farm.
How many *alphabets* are there in English?	How many *alphabet* are there in English?
I cannot understand your *logics.*	I cannot understand your *logic.*
He received a prize for his *needle works.*	He received a prize for his *needle work.*
His *woodworks* were very much admired.	His *woodwork* was very much admired.

Note : 'Rices', 'corns', 'foods' are used to denote different kinds of rice, corn, food and not a large quantity of these items. Similarly 'advice', 'scenery', 'hair', 'offspring', 'furniture', etc., do not take 's' after them unless the other meaning of the word is intended. 'Advice' means counsel, but 'advices' means information, 'sceneries' denote different kind of scenery. 'Hairs' is used when attention is drawn to number. 'Abuses' denotes evil practices and is not a term of abuse.

The following nouns are alike in the singular and the plural : 'Sheep', 'deer', 'fish', 'pice', 'trout', 'cod', 'salmon', 'series', 'species', 'canon', 'urine', 'corps', etc.

Note : The following nouns are always used in the plural :

'Bellows', 'precincts', 'tongs', 'shoes', 'socks', 'stockings', 'trousers', 'scissors', 'fetters', 'spectacles', 'shears', 'pyjamas', 'pants', 'glanders', 'billiards', 'cards', 'draughts', 'bowels', 'entrails', 'annals', 'thanks', 'remains', 'contents', 'savings', 'lodgings', 'proceeds', 'assets', 'victuals', 'premises', 'aims', 'riches', 'auspices', 'cares', 'innings', 'quarters', 'nuptials', 'ashes', 'tidings', 'breeches', 'drawers', 'wages', 'embers', 'measles' 'tactics', 'surroundings', 'dregs', 'intestines', 'pincers', 'letters' (meaning *learning*), 'eaves', etc.

Note : The following are the nouns which are plural in form, but are used as singular : 'News', 'runnings', 'alms', 'amends', 'gallows', 'Mathematics', 'Physics', 'Politics', 'Ethics', 'Gymnastics', 'Dynamics', 'summons', (the plural is 'summonses'), 'means' (meaning wealth), etc.

Note : Nouns expressing number and weight (when preceded by numerals) are not pluralised, as : 'two *pair* of shoes'; 'five *dozen* of apples'; 'two *score* of mangoes'; 'five *head* of cattle', 'two *hundred* rupees', 'twelve *stone* weight', 'four *yoke* of oxen', 'three *thousand* rupees', 'a three-*mile* race', 'a *five-yard* piece of cloth', etc.

But we say : '*Hundreds* of boys came to watch the match.' 'There were *thousands* of people in the fair.'

Examples

Incorrect	*Correct*
He told *these news* to his brother.	He told *this news* to his brother.
Have you packed your *luggages.*	Have you packed your *luggage.*
There are no *breads* in the kitchen.	There is no *bread* in the kitchen.
Please excuse the *troubles.*	Please excuse the *trouble.*
He took *troubles* to achieve this purpose.	He took *trouble* to achieve the purpose.
In Delhi there are many *poors.*	In Delhi there are many *poor* (or *poor men*).
He provided the *blinds* with money.	He provided the *blind* with money.
This tree bears no *fruits.*	This tree bears no *fruit.*
Mohan has gone to Delhi for further *study.*	Mohan has gone to Delhi for further *studies.*
His *merits* are exceptional.	His *merit* is exceptional.
His talk on the advantages of foreign *travels* was much appreciated.	His talk on the advantages of foreign *travel* was much appreciated.
You should not find *faults* with my work.	You should not find *fault* with my work.
We shall get over the difficulty of the *finance.*	We shall get over the difficulty of the *finances.*
The *materials* for my work could not be secured.	The *material* for my work could not be secured.

Nouns that take 's' after them :

He should wear light-coloured *pant* (or *trouser*).	He should wear light-coloured *pants* (or *trousers*).
He purchased a pair of *sock*.	He purchased a pair of *socks*.
My *circumstance* does not permit me to spend more.	My *circumstances* do not permit me to spend more.
The *order* was issued by the commander.	The *orders* were issued by the commander.
I took my *meal* at 11 A.M.	I took my *meals* at 11 A.M.
He bought *vegetable* from the market.	He bought *vegetables* from the market.
Mathematic is difficult to learn.	*Mathematics* is difficult to learn.

Note : 'Mathematics', 'Physics', 'Optics', 'Mechanics', 'Gymnastics', 'Politics', etc.—These words always take 's' after them, but they take singular Verbs.

Note : There are other nouns that always take a plural form and a plural verb.

Note : There are some nouns that have the same form in singular as well as plural e.g. : 'score', 'deer', 'swine', 'cannon', 'fish', 'salmon', 'sheep', 'grass', etc.

Note : Certain collective nouns preceded by a numeral do not take 's' after them.

Man' counsels were briefed.	*Many counsel* were briefed.

We had *two dozens* of eggs.	We had *two dozen* of eggs.
We had *several dozens* of eggs.	We had *several dozen* of eggs.
Six pairs of oxen were bought.	*Six pair* of oxen were bought.

Note : The collective nouns, in the following examples, though singular in form are always used in plural : (1) The *cattle* are grazing. (2) The *gentry* have been invited. (3) My *poultry* have made me rich. (4) The *people* of our village *are* rich. (5) Mankind *want* peace. (6) The peasantry of India *are* industrious. (7) The vermin are killed. (8) The clergy were present. (9)The *police* were sent on the track.

Note : When 'people' is used as a common noun, it is used both in the singular and the plural.

The Indians are a simple and brave *people.*

The *peoples* (nations) of Asia are making rapid progress.

Note : Proper, abstract and material nouns have no plural except when they are used as common nouns :

Examples

Incorrect	*Correct*
This house is built of *bricks*, not of *stones.*	This house is built of *brick*, not of *stone.*
I ran a *five-miles* race.	I ran a *five-mile* race.
The two leaders had a *two-hours* talk.	The two leaders had a *two-hour* talk

A *five-men* delegation waited as the Prime Minister. . .	A *five-man* delegation waited as the Prime Minister. . .

Note : When a noun is made to do the work of an Adjective in a compound word, it should not be used in the plural form : 'a hundred-yard race', 'a ten-rupee note', 'two-hour talk', 'a ten-year old boy', 'an eight-anna piece', 'a ten-pound weight', 'a five-year plan', 'a three-hour talk', 'seven-day week', etc.

We say '*pieces* of poetry', 'pieces of advice', 'pieces of art' and 'articles of clothing', 'articles of baggage', 'articles of furniture'. 'Fishes' denotes different kinds of fish ; 'hairs', different kinds of hair.

Note : Some nouns have two forms in the plural, each with a different meaning, as :

Brother :

(*i*) Brothers : Sons of the same parents
(*ii*) Brethren : Members of the same community

Cloth :

(*i*) Cloths : Kinds of pieces of cloth
(*ii*) Clothes : Garments

Die :

(*i*) Dies : Stamps for coining
(*ii*) Dice : Small cubes in a game

Genius :

(*i*) Geniuses : Person of great talent
(*ii*) Genii : Spirits

Index :

(*i*) Indexes : Tables of contents
(*ii*) Indices : Sign used in Algebra

Staff :

(*i*) Staffs : Sticks

(*ii*) Staff : A body of clerks or teachers

Possessive Case

Note : The apostrophe 's' after a noun is added only in the case of animate objects, not in the case of inanimate, *except after expressions which denote :* (*i*) time; (*ii*) weight; (*iii*) distance. e.g. : 'An hour's talk', 'a maund's weight', 'A mile's distance', 'a stone's throw', 'a week's leave', 'a needle's point', etc.

Incorrect	*Correct*
I had an *hour talk* with him.	I had an *hour's talk* with him
I covered *a distance of mile.*	I covered a *mile's distance.*
He arrived on *Monday's night.*	He arrived on *Monday night.*
Our *summer's vacations* (or holidays) commence soon.	Our *summer vacations* (or holidays) commence soon.
He is going on a *month leave.*	He is going on a *month's leave.*
It is a *day journey* between Ludhiana and Delhi.	It is a *day's journey* between Ludhiana and Delhi.
This is a *book of Rama.*	This is *Rama's b ook.*

Note : To change a plural noun into possessive case remember that

(*i*) If it denotes person (like 'man', 'ladies', etc.), and does not end in 's', then apostrophe 's' is added to it, e.g. 'Men's garments'; 'children's books'; etc.

(*ii*) Nouns showing the personified objects also take apostrophe 's', e.g. : 'India's heroes', 'Death's toll', 'life's burden', etc.

(*iii*) Apostrophe 's' is also used in the following familiar phrases : 'At his wits' end'; 'to his heart's content', 'out of harm's way', 'a bird's-eye view', etc

(*iv*) Only an apostrophe (') is used in the cases of the plural nouns that end in 's', e.g. : 'boys' school', 'girls' college', 'Moses' Law', 'for goodness' sake', etc.

Today I will dine at my *uncle's house*.	Today I will dine at my uncle's.

Note : The words : 'house', 'church', 'school', 'shop', etc., are often omitted after possessive case.

My *uncle's secretary's wife* died yesterday.	The *wife of my uncle's secretary* died yesterday.
One of the travellers' sons was killed.	*The son of one of the travellers* was killed.

Note : Avoid the use of double possessive.

Neither did *his* efforts bear fruit nor did *your's*.	Neither did *his* efforts bear fruits nor did *yours*.

Note : The words, 'his', 'hers', 'its', 'theirs', 'yours', 'ours', etc., are possessive. They are neither written within the possessive sign (') nor are followed by nouns.

It is a *girls's* college.	It is a *girls'* college.

Note : When a noun is plural and ends in 's , the possessive case is formed by adding only an apostrophe, e.g. : 'boys' school', 'girls' college', 'horses' tail', etc. Do not use two 's'.

This is a *ladies's* park.	This is a *ladies'* park.

Note: When the noun is plural and does not end in 's' the possessive case is formed by adding only an apostrophe, e.g. : 'boys' school', 'girls' college', 'horses' tail', etc. Do not use two 's'.

This is a *womens* park.	This is a *women's* park.

Note : When the noun is plural and does not end in 's', the possessive case is formed by adding apostrophe e.g. : 'men's club', 'children's park', 'women's hostel', etc.

COMMON ERRORS IN THE USE OF NOUNS

Incorrect	*Correct*
I spent the holidays with my *family members*.	I spent the holidays with my *family* (or I spent the holidays with *members of my family*).
There is no more *place* in this compartment.	There is no more *room* in this compartment.
Bring me the *blotting*.	Bring me the *blotting paper*.
What are you writing in your *copy*.	What are you writing in your *notebook*.
Our *boarding* is not yet full.	Our *boarding house* is not yet full.

I am reading a new *poetry*.	I am reading a new *poem*.
Give my *B.C.* (or *compliments*) to all.	Convey my *kind*(*est*) *regards* to all.
Did he hit an *over boundary*.	Did he hit *a six*.
Are there any more waiting members in your *party*.	Are there any more waiting members (or reserves) on your *side* (or in your *team*).
There was a *joker* at the circus.	There was a *clown* at the circus.
We did not have a *good play* of football.	We did not have a *good game* of football.
We saw a *theatre*.	We saw a *play*.
He does not like taking part in a *drama*.	He does not like acting in a *play*.
He is a short-statured *gentleman*.	He is a short-statured *man*.
There are two *females* sitting in the compartment.	There are two *women* sitting in the compartment.
He was wearing a new *dress*.	He was wearing a new *suit*.
He took no *insult* at this.	He took no *offence* at this.
The almirah contains books, papers and *others*.	The almirah contains books, papers and *such things*.
He did not put his *signs* on this paper.	He did not put his *signatures* on this paper.
He is my *cousin brother*.	He is my *cousin*.
We are all *fellow brothers*.	We are all *brothers*.
Did you *pass the noon* at study.	Did you *spend the middle part* of the day at study.

He had a *great number* of money.	He had a *good amount* of money.
He got to a *bad companionship*.	He got into *bad company*.
The *front* (or *back*) of my house is not in good condition.	The *front side* (or *back side*) of my house is not in a good condition.
I could not *take a bath* in the sea.	I could not *have a bath* in the sea.
He hurt his *foot finger*.	He hurt *his toe*.
The gentry of the town *was* invited to the feast.	The gentry of the town *were* invited to the feast.
I like *fruits and vegetables*.	I like *fruit and vegetables*.
He has no male *issues*.	He has no male *issue*.
You must continue your *study*.	You must continue your *studies*.
Summer *vacations are* near.	Summer *vacation is* near. (one term)
Politics *are* a dirty game.	Politics *is* a dirty game.
My *mean is* limited.	My *means are* limited.
He told the story in details.	He told the story in *detail*.
He purchased a *ground*.	He purchased a *plot of ground*.
His *wage is* low.	His *wages are* low.
We have already had our *meal*.	We have already had our *meals*.
Tender my *respect* to him.	Tender my *respects* to him.
The population of this village is five *thousands*.	The population of this village is five *thousand*.

The earthquake did *many damages.*	The earthquake did *much damage.*
There was a letter *on the ground* of this room.	There was a letter *on the floor* of this room.
I was in the *centre* of the room.	I was in the *middle* of the room.
I returned to my home late *in* night.	I returned to my home *at* night.
The *weather* of Dalhousie is very nice.	The *climate* of Dalhousie is very nice.
There is a tree *in the front side of* our college.	There is a tree *in front of* our college.
There is a temple *at the back side of* our college.	There is a temple *at the back of* our college.
He wears a silk dress.	He wears a *silk suit.*
I have secured an *employment* in this office.	I have secured an *appointment* in this office.
What are your *fooding* expenses.	What are your *food* expenses.
We are *fellow brothers.*	We are *brethren* (or *brothers*).
The market was *full of men.*	The market was *full of people.*
Please grant me *one day leave.*	Please grant me *one day's leave.*
He weights about *ten stones.*	He weighs about *ten stone.*
We use *woods* as fuel.	We use *wood* as fuel.
The *sister of my friend* is the hostess.	*My friend's sister* is the hostess.
The *house's walls* are damaged	The *walls of the house* are damaged.
Even animals love their *offsprings.*	Even animals love their *offspring.*

She reached the age of *two scores* and one.	She reached the age of *two score* and one.
Five B.A. and *two M.A.* applied for the job.	Five *B.A.'s* and two *M.A.'s* applied for the job.
I gave *two pices* to the beggar.	I gave *two pice* to the beggar.
My *scissor is* blunt.	My *scissors are* blunt.
He needs a *spectacles.*	He needs *a pair of spectacles.*
His hair *are* white.	His hair *is* white.
I want *two breads.*	I want two *loaves* (or *two pieces*) *of bread.*
Neither did his efforts bear fruit nor did *your's.*	Neither did his efforts bear fruit nor did *yours.*
He has *no issues.*	He has *no issue.*
He gave me *many* informations.	He gave me *much* information.
He did *many mischiefs.*	He did *many acts of mischief.*
Entry to the cinema will be by *tickets.*	Entry to the cinema will be by *ticket.*
He has *five grey hair.*	He has five grey *hairs.*
Her appearance is just like her *mother.*	Her appearance is just like her *mother's.*
Tell me the *content* of this letter.	Tell me the *contents* of this letter.
He provided the *blinds* with clothes.	He provided the *blind* with clothes.
My *thank is* due to him.	My *thanks are* due to him.
I received glad *tiding* of his success.	I received glad *tidings* of his success.
I bought a *land.*	I bought a *plot of land.*

CHAPTER II

PRONOUNS

Incorrect	*Correct*
I, you and he have done the work.	*You, he and I* have done the work.
Mohan and I have spoiled this book.	I and *Mohan have* spoiled this book.

Note : 'I' comes last, when 'you' and 'he' *are* mentioned in the same sentence, but in admitting a fault, 'I' (the first person) comes first.

I will send him to *your's.*	I will send him to *your house.*

Note : 'Yours' is correct if the word 'house' has already been used, as in 'He came to my house and then went to yours.'

He is not *such* a rogue *that* would do it.	He is not *such* a rouge *as* would do it.
I *feel myself ill* today.	I *feel ill* today.
Suffice to say I cannot work more.	*Suffice it to say* I cannot work more.
Those who attended yesterday should get *yourselves* marked present.	Those who attended yesterday should get *themselves* marked present.

It is hard to bear *your separation.*	It is hard to bear *separation from you.*
I beg to take *your leave.*	I beg to take *leave of you.*
One should not shirk *his* duty.	One should not shirk one's duty.
Which of you would like to give *your* book.	Which of you would like to give *his* (or her) book.
His very sight annoyed me.	*The very sight of him* annoyed me.
He is the best speaker *who* could be found in the college.	He is the best speaker *that* could be found in the college.
I am not buying an article *that* does not suit me.	I am not buying an article *which* does not suit me.

Note : 'Which' conveys additional information somewhat new, and 'that' merely explains and defines a certain thing or statement.

Incorrect	*Correct*
Each of these men *read* books.	Each of these men *reads* books.
Both could not pass in the examination.	*Neither of them could* pass in the examinations.
We all could not reach there in time.	*None of us could* reach there in time.
Here is my letter, *please read.*	Here is my letter, *please read it.*
'Have you a book?' 'I have not *got.*'	'Have you a book?' 'No, I have not *got one.*
'Is he doing his work?' 'Yes, *I think.*'	'Is he doing his work?' 'Yes, I *think so.*'
He *enjoyed* during the summer vacation.	He *enjoyed himself* during the summer vacation.

The boy who comes out first, *he* will get a prize.	The boy who comes out first will get a prize.
Whoever does best in the examination, *he* will get a prize.	Whoever does best in the examination will get a prize.

Note : The vernacular idiom is responsible for the mistakes in sentences as given above.

'Who wrote this?' 'Myself.'	'Who wrote this?' '*I*' (myself).
I and he are cousins.	*He and I* are cousins.
I with some friends went for a walk.	I went for a walk with some friends.

Note : A pronoun used as subject should not be separated from its verb if possible.

He is wiser than *me*.	He is wiser than *I*.
The inspector *tested the class if it could* reply to his question.	The inspector *tested if* the *class could* reply to his question.

Note : The object of 'tested' is not 'class', but the whole noun clause.

You should see the cycle whether it works well.	You should see whether the cycle works well.
None of us *have* done work.	None of us *has* done work.

Note : 'Every', 'each', 'none', 'much', 'person' are singular words; 'all', 'some', 'most', many 'people' are plurals.

Every one was surprised when *they* saw such a large elephant.	Every one was surprised when *he* saw such a large elephant.

<table>
<tr><td>The size of my new coat should be same as the previous coat.</td><td>The size of my new coat should be the same as that of the previous coat.</td></tr>
<tr><td>My rooms are better than my brother.</td><td>My rooms are better than that of my brother.</td></tr>
<tr><td>Either of these books will be suitable for me.</td><td>Any of these books will be suitable for me.</td></tr>
<tr><td>Any of these two boys can come.</td><td>Either of these two boys can come.</td></tr>
</table>

Note : 'Either' is used for two things, 'any' is used for more than two.

<table>
<tr><td>The boy is my cousin who stood first in the mile race.</td><td>The boy, who stood first in the mile race, is my cousin.</td></tr>
<tr><td>The house has a beautiful situation, which was built newly.</td><td>The house, which was built newly had a beaütiful situation.</td></tr>
</table>

Note : The relative pronoun should be placed as near as possible to its antecedent, so that no ambiguity may arise.

<table>
<tr><td>I will find out the student whom, I learn has been expelled from the university.</td><td>I will find out the student who, I learn has been expelled from the university.</td></tr>
<tr><td>Neither Ram nor Sohan are responsible for this mistake.</td><td>Neither Ram nor Sohan is responsible for this mistake.</td></tr>
<tr><td>Either Karim or Mohammed have done this work</td><td>Either Karim or Mohammed has done this work.</td></tr>
</table>

Note : When two or more singular nouns are joined by either or, neither nor, the pronouns are generally used in singular.

Each man and each boy *are* responsible for their actions.	Each man and each boy *is* responsible for his action.

Note : When two singular nouns, joined by 'and', are preceded by 'each' or 'every', the pronoun used for them is in the singular.

Either the guard or the engine drivers *is* responsible for this accident.	Either the guard or the engine drivers *are* responsible for this accident.

Note : If a plural and a singular noun are joined by either or, neither nor, the pronoun and verb used should be in the plural.

You, Mohan and I *has* always done our duty.	You, Mohan and I *have* always done our duty.
You and he *is* always sitting at home.	You and he *are* always sitting at home.

Note : When pronouns of different persons are joined by 'and' and used as the subject of a sentence, the verb is used in plural.

I, *he* and *you* shall go together.	*You*, *he* and *I* shall go together.
I and *you* are never absent from the class.	*You* and *I* are never absent from the class.
I and *he* must reach the station in time.	*He* and *I* must reach the station in time.

You and *he* are thieves. *He* and *you* are thieves.

Note : When there are pronouns of different persons, second person should come first, third person next and first person last, unless used in pejorative sense (like in the last sentence above), when the order is reversed.

Usage of 'None'

'None' is used in the singular when it points to a material noun, e.g. : 'I want some sugar, there is *none* in the pot.'

'None' is used in the singular or plural form when it points to persons or common nouns; e.g. : 'Is there any message for me ?' 'No, there is *none*' (*singular*). '*None* but the hard working deserve the price'. 'Do you want mangoes ?' 'There are *none* in the basket.'

Note : Use of '*each*', '*everyone*', '*everybody*' (plural) 'everybody', 'everyone', 'nobody'

Note : The pronouns 'his', 'her' are used for 'each', 'everyone', etc. according to reference.

Each of these boys has done *his* composition work.

Everyone of the ladies purchased a new sari for *herself*.

Note : When the gender (masculine or feminine) is not expressed, 'he' is used.

Everyone in the meeting expressed *his* views.

Everybody must obey *his* parents.

Anyone can become rich, if *he* works hard.

Note : The relative pronoun is some time omitted in the objective case :

I am the monarch of all/I survey. ('that' is omitted)
I have lost the book/you gave me. ('that' is omitted)

Note : The antecedent of a relative pronoun is some time omitted :

Whom the gods love die young=Those whom the gods love die young.

Who laughs last laughs best = He who laughs last laughs best.

Note : A relative pronoun should agree with its antecedent in number and person ; as—

It is I who am in fault.

The boys who are lazy are punished.

Incorrect	*Correct*
It is *me.*	It is *I.*
This is between you and *I.*	This is between you and *me.*
Nobody was there but *I.*	Nobody was there but *me.*
One should respect *his* elders.	One should respect *one's* elders.
Let you and *I* go to the pictures.	Let you and *me* go to the pictures.
He is stronger than *me.*	He is stronger than *I.*
This pen is better than *your.*	This pen is better than *yours.*
He came with Satish and *myself.*	He came with Satish and *me.*
Who is *clever* ? Mohan or Sohan ?	Who is the *cleverer*, Mohan or Sohan ?

Who did you see ?	*Whom* did you see ?
Tell me what *is he.*	Tell me what *he is.*
Tell me whom *did you meet* yesterday.	Tell me whom *you met* yesterday.
Such girls *who* were absent were fined.	*Such* girls *as* were absent were fined.
The committee *was* divided in its opinion.	The committee *were* divided in their opinion.
You and Sheila *has* done her work.	You and Sheila *have* done your work.
Your's sincerely.	*Yours* sincerely.
We must now take *his leave.*	We must now take *leave of him.*
This is the chair *whose leg* was broken today.	This is the chair *the leg of which* was broken today.
He is taller than *me.*	He is taller than *I.*
This is the table *whose price* is very cheap	This is the table *the price of which* is very cheap.

Note : Generally 'whose' is used for denoting persons, and 'which' for denoting lifeless objects.

Please give me the book. I am giving *it.*	Please give me the book. I am giving ('it' is omitted.)

Note : Sometime the pronoun 'it' is omitted, where it is needed.

Who did you abuse ?	*Whom* did you abuse ?
Whom do you think got the prize ?	*Who* do you think got the prize ?

Note : 'Who' denotes subject and 'whom' stands for object.

Between you and *I* , he is going to face a debacle	Between you and *me*, he is going to face a debacle.

Note : The object of a verb or of a preposition, when it is a pronoun, should be of the objective form.

He went there and *enjoyed*.	He went there and *enjoyed himself*.

Note : When such verbs as 'avail', 'absent', 'enjoy', 'apply', 'resign', 'acquit', 'drink', 'over-reach', 'exert', 'oversleep', 'revenge', 'set', 'distinguish', are used reflexively, never omit the reflexive pronoun.

We *kept ourselves away* from the college.	We *kept away* from the college.
I *qualified myself* for the profession.	I *qualified* for this profession.

Note : The following verbs—'qualify', 'rest,' 'enlist', 'break', 'bathe', 'dash', 'keep', 'move', 'make', 'spread', 'draw', 'roll', 'burst', 'hide', 'feel', 'form', 'gather', 'lengthen', 'marry', 'open', 'repent', 'stop', 'steal'—are not followed by reflexive pronouns.

It was *him* who did it.	It was *he* who did it.
If I were *him*, I would not go there.	If I were *he*, I would not go there.

Note : The complement of the verb 'to be', when it is expressed by a pronoun, should be in the nominative form.

Nobody will be allowed to express *their* views.	Nobody will be allowed to express *his* views.
The firm has given a gift to each of *their* clerk.	The firm has given a gift to each of *its* clerk.
Who are you speaking to.	*Whom* are you speaking to.

Note : A pronoun which is governed by a preposition must be in the objective case. Hence "whom".

Will you take a cup of tea ?	Will you take a cup of tea ?
Thanks, I do not need.	Thanks, I do not need it.

Note : A pronoun should not be omitted when it takes the place of a noun in the objective case after a transitive verb.

Both *himself* and *Sham* did it.	Both *he* and *Sham* did it.
He and *myself* went to cinema	*He* and *I* went to cinema.
Myself saw him do this.	*I* saw him do this.
He made *your mention.*	He made a *mention of you.*
I hope to receive *your good report.*	I hope to receive *a good report of you.*

Note : A noun or pronoun in the possessive case should not be used as the antecedent to a relative pronoun.

He is richer than *me.*	He is richer than *I* (am).
You are abler than *him.*	You are abler than *he* (is).

Note : When a pronoun follows 'than' the case of such a pronoun is to be determined from the content.

Some Examples

I am glad at my *mother* *coming.*	I am glad at my *mother's* *coming.*
Is it *me* you wish to see ?	Is it *I* you wish to see ?
Who did this ? Myself.	Who did this ? *I* did it.
They have no houses of *theirs.*	They have no houses of *their own.*
This is the bird *who* sings.	This is the bird *that* sings.
Everyone must do *one's* best.	Everyone must do *his* best.
I am *yours* obedient servant.	I am *your* obedient servant (or yours obediently).
He works harder than *me.*	He works harder than *I.*
Both did not study.	*Neither studied.*
We all did not study.	*None of us* studied.
None of us *have* met him.	None of us *has* met him.
Your's sincerely or your sincerely.	Yours sincerely (or *your sincere friend*).
He told the story to *whoever* he met.	He told the story to *whomever* he met.
His teaching is *like* Gandhi.	His teaching is *like that of* Gandhi.
He is one of the greatest *man* who *has* ever lived.	He is one of the greatest *men* who *have* ever lived.
I, *you* and *he* are in the list.	*You*, *he* and *I* are in the list.
Neither of them *were* paid for.	Neither of them *was* paid for.

He said that *I am* going.	He said that *he was* going.
Sohan and Mohan love *one another*.	Sohan and Mohan love *each other*.
Such boys, *who* do not work hard, fail.	Such boys, *as* do not work hard, fail.
Both Ram as well as his brother came to see her.	Both Ram and his brother (or Ram as well as his brother) came to see her.

Note : Either use 'both' or 'as well as'.

Mohan as well as Sham *are* there.	Mohan as well as Sham *is* there.

Note : Two singular subjects joined by 'as well as' require the predicate verb to be singular.

Either my friend or I are visiting the place.	Either my friend or I shall be visiting the place.

Note : When any two subjects, not of the same person, are joined by 'or' or 'nor', the verb agrees with the subject nearest it.

Neither he nor she *have* gone there.	Neither he nor she *has* gone there.

Note : Singular subjects connected by 'or' or 'nor' need a singular verb.

Neither he nor his brothers *is* to blame.	Neither he nor his brothers *are* to blame.

Note : In using 'neither', 'either', the verb should follow the second noun or pronoun.

Myself saw him do this.	*I* saw him do this.
This is the best *which* we could do.	This is the best *that* we could do.
He made *your mention.*	He made *a mention of you.*

Note : A noun or pronoun in the possessive case should not be used as the antecedent to a relative pronoun.

I have read Byron's poetry who was a lover of Nature.	I have read the poetry of Byron who was a lover of Nature.
It is the system, not the individual, which I criticise.	It is the system, which I criticise, not the individual.

Note : A relative pronoun or the relative adverb should be placed as close to its antecedent as possible.

They that are intelligent have no need of a tutor.	Those that are intelligent have no need of a tutor.
You are abler than *him.*	You are abler than *he* (is).
He is richer than *me.*	He is richer than *I* (am).

Note : When a pronoun follows, then the case of such a pronoun is to be determined from the content.

I was glad at my *mother coming.*	I was glad at my *mother's coming.*

Please excuse *me being late.*	Please excuse *my being late.*

Note : A noun or pronoun governing a geround should be put in the possessive case. None should be put with 's'.

We feel happy at them coming.	We feel happy at their coming.

Note : A noun or pronoun denoting a person or some other living being must be in the possessive case when placed before a gerund.

Is it *me* you wish to see?	Is it *I* you wish to see?
All but *him* had fled.	All but *he* had fled.
He told the story to *whoever* he met.	He told the story to *whosoever* he met.
Our game is hockey, their is tennis.	Our game is hockey, theirs is tennis.

Adjectives

Mohan is best speaker of all. — Mohan is *the* best speaker of all.

Ram is wiser than all students. — Ram is wiser than all *other* students.

This man appears to have seen *more happier* days. — This man appears to have seen *happier* days.

Note : Double comparative is wrong.

This type of magazine is *more preferable* to that. — This type of magazine *is preferable* to that.

His work is *superior than* his brothers. — His work is *superior to* his brothers.

Note : Comparatives ending in —'ior'—take 'to' and not 'than' after them.

Neither of these five persons came to see me. — *None* of these five persons came to see me.

Note : 'Neither' and 'either' are used for two objects.

Either of you eight can take up this work. — *Any* of you eight can take up this work.

Wealth and wine are both temptations, *this* makes one proud, *that* upsets his system. — Wealth and wine are both temptations, *that* makes one proud, *this* upsets his system.

Mohan and Sohan are equally to blame; *this* continued the fault, *that* committed it.	Mohan and Sohan are equally to blame; *that* continued the fault, *this* committed it.

Note : When 'this' and 'that', 'former' and 'latter', 'one' and 'other' refer to two objects previously mentioned, 'this , 'one', 'latter', refer to the second of them, and that 'other' and 'former' refer to the first.

He gets only *passing* marks in all subjects.	He gets only *pass* marks in the subjects.
Today I feel somewhat *uneasy.*	Today I feel somewhat *unwell.*

Note : 'Uneasy' denotes restlessness of the mental state.

I have a *strong* headache.	I have a *bad* headache.
Krishan is *an obedient and respectful boy* to his parents.	Krishan is *a boy, obedient* and *respectful to* his parents.
An obedient servant to the master is always successful.	*A servant obedient* to the master is always successful.

Note : When an adjective is connected with other words, it comes after the noun.

Ram is my *older* brother.	Ram is my *elder* brother.

Note : 'Elder', 'eldest', are used for persons, 'older', 'oldest' for inanimate objects.

This tree is the *eldest* one here.	This tree is the *oldest* one here.
The rain wa s *plenty* there.	The rain was *plentiful* there.

There were no *less* than fifteen girls there.	There were no *fewer* than fifteen girls there.

Note : 'Less' denotes degree, quantity; 'fewer' denotes number.

Incorrect	*Correct*
It is *worthwhile* going there.	It is *worth* going there.
Did *somebody* go there ?	Did *anybody* go there ?
I was glad to *learn* this news.	I was glad to *hear* this news.
Cut this melon into *two* halves.	Cut this melon *into halves* (or *in half*).
You should read the *two first* chapters.	You should read the *first two* chapters.
The three boys will help *each other.*	The three boys will help *one another.*
Trees stood on *either side* of the road.	Trees stood on *each side* (or *both sides*) of the road.
The *first two* boys will get the prize.	The *two first* boys will get the prize.
Every people know fully well about the happening.	*Everyone knows* fully well about the happening.
He held the chair *in the both* hands.	He held the chair *in both* hands (or both his hands).
Both of them have not come.	*Neither of them has* come.
Kalidas is greater than any other *poets* in the world.	Kalidas is greater than any other *poet* in the world.
Open your book at *ten page.*	Open your book at *page ten.*

He is in *class tenth.*	He is in *class ten.* (Or *the tenth class.*)
The book cost me *rupees five.*	The book cost me *five rupees.*
Mohan is *elder* that I.	Mohan is *older* than I.
Krishan gets a *less* salary.	Krishan gets a *small* salary.
Among the two he is *cleverer.*	He is the *more clever of the two.*
He is *more* handsome *than the others.*	He is the *most* handsome *of all others.*
The enemy is becoming *strong.*	The enemy is becoming *stronger.*
There is a *best* tailor in this street.	There is a *very good* tailor in this street.
There is a *worth seeing sight* in Delhi.	There is a *sight worth seeing* in Delhi.
I intend spending my *future life/remaining life* in Kashmir.	I intend spending *the rest of my life* in Kashmir.
He obtained leave *of ten days.*	He obtained *ten days' leave*; or *leave for ten days.*
I am *hopeless to get* through the examination.	I have *no hope of getting* through the examination.
She was so *big lady* that she could not get up from the chair.	She was so *big a lady* that she could not get up from the chair.
Your affectionate friend.	*Yours* affectionate friend or *yours* affectionately.
Your loving friend.	*Yours loving* friend.
This area in the district is *plain.*	This area in the district is *level* or *flat.*

He obtained nearly *cent per cent* marks.	He obtained nearly *full* marks.
The gold is yellow.	*Gold* is yellow.
Mohan attended the *society* function.	Mohan attended the *social* function.
We should love *the* Nature.	We should love Nature.
Each and every person wore a Gandhi cap.	*Each person/Everybody* wore a Gandhi cap.

Note : 'Each' and 'every' can be used together correctly to convey very strong emphasis. Usually one of the two objectives is quite sufficient.

He is a *coward/miser* man.	He is a *cowardly/miserly* man.
The police had *sifting* inquiry.	The police had a *thorough* inquiry.
Mohan got *few* marks in the examination.	Mohan got *a few* marks in the examination.

Note : 'A few' means some. It is positive. 'Few' means nothing. 'A little' means something. 'Little' means nothing or nought.

I can offer you *few* rupees that are in my pocket.	I can offer you *a few* rupees that are in my pocket.
This is the *latter* edition published on Gandhi.	This is the *later* edition published on Gandhl.
Sohan and Mohan were playing when the *later* got hurt.	Sohan and Mohan were playing when the *latter* got hurt.

Note : 'Latter' means mentioned later in order.

The station is *further* from my house than it is from yours.	The station is *farther* from my house than it is from yours.

Note : 'Farther' is used for distance. 'Further' means additional.

These are *farther* remarks that I wish to make on the subject.	These are *further* remarks that I wish to make on the subject.
Mohan's statement is more *right* than Sohan's.	Mohan's statement is more *correct* than Sohan's.

Note : There are some adjectives which are not used in comparative or superlative degrees such as 'preferable', 'extreme', 'right', 'supreme', 'square', 'unique', 'round', 'perfect', 'universal', 'unchangeable', 'golden', 'eternal', 'ideal', 'entire', 'complete'.

Sheila's pen is inferior *than* Leela's.	Sheila's pen is inferior *to* Leela's.
My rights are prior *than* Krishan's.	My rights are prior *to* Krishan's.
All the class left the room.	*The whole* class left the room.

Note : 'All' refers to number. 'Whole' refers to quantity.

Many *a jokes were* cut during the conversation.	Many *a joke was* cut during the conversation.

Note : 'Many', 'much', 'many a' : 'Many' denotes a number and 'much' denotes quantity, 'Many a' means—many times one thing. It is followed by a singular noun and takes a singular verb.

Mohan possesses little money that he wishes to spend.	Mohan possesses *a* little money that he wishes to spend.
Krishan is out of pockets. He is penniless and has *a* little money.	Krishan is out of pocket. He is penniless and has little money.
Vimla and Shanti helped *one another*.	Vimla and Shanti helped *each other*.
Rich should help *poors*.	Rich should help the *poor*.
I would leave by the *latest* train.	I would leave by the *last* train.
I have no *rupee*.	I have no *money*.
The climate *of plain* is better *than* mountains.	The climate of *the plains* is better *than that of* the mountains.
He is cleverest of *all other* boys.	He is *the* cleverest of *all* boys.
He is the poorest of *any student* in the college.	He is the poorest of *all* the *students* in the college.
The Tribune has the largest circulation *than* any newspaper.	*The Tribune* has the largest circulation *of all* newspapers. Or *The Tribune* has the larger circulation *than any other* newspaper.

Note : In the comparative degree use "any other

than". In the superlative degree do not use "any other than" but use 'the' before, and "of all" after the superlative.

He is richer than wise.	He is *more* rich than wise.

Note : The 'er' sign of the comparative is not used when two qualities of the same thing or person are to be compared.

He is the richest and honest man.	He is the richest and *most* honest man.

Note : When two adjectives refer to the same subject and one of them is superlative, the other must also be superlative.

It is *much* hot today.	It is *very* hot today.
He sat *nearest* to me.	He sat *next* to me.
This mango tastes *sourly*.	This mango tastes *sour*.
He was present on *both* days.	He was present on *both the* days.

Note : When 'both' is used as an adjective, it should be followed by 'the'. With possessive pronoun or noun, it should come before, and not after.

I have *not* any books.	I have *no* books (or I *do not have any* books).

Note : The phrase 'not any' or 'no any' is wrong.

Work *only* fills our life with joy.	Work *alone* fills our life with joy.

Note : 'Only' is an adverb.

He wrote a *best* book.	He wrote a *very good* book.
She has *the best* voice *of* any singer.	She has *better* voice *than* any other singer.
He is *rather* richer than his friend.	He is *richer* than his friend.

Note : "Rather" has force of comparative. Double comparatives should not be used.

Sham is *braver* than wise.	Sham is *more brave* than wise.

Note : The comparative in 'er' is not used when we compare two qualities in the same person or thing. In that case we use 'more' before the adjective.

I gave her *any* book.	I gave her *some* book.
I will not buy *some* book.	I will not buy *any* book.
Please run *fastly.*	Please run *fast,*
He has no other *friends except* Sham.	He has no other *friend than* Sham.
My sister is two years *old* than *me.*	My sister is two years *elder* than *I* (or *elder to me* by two years).
Less books are needed now.	*Fewer* books are needed now.
He is *sick* in appearance.	He is *sickly* in appearance.
I consider it a *great* luck.	I consider it a *good* luck.
No poet is as great as Tagore.	*No other* poet is as great as Tagore.

Articles

He lent *me few* rupees.

He lent *me a few* rupees.

There are great many trees in that jungle.

There are *a* great many trees in that jungle.

Recent occurrences in Punjab were condemned by the government.

The recent occurences in the Punjab were condemned by the government.

A *brave man and an accomplished officer* published his account of the war.

A *brave and accomplished* officer published his account of the war.

Note : When two adjectives refer to one person the verb is singular and the article is not repeated.

The Doctor, Musician and Professor were seen sitting together.

The Doctor, *the* Musician and *the* Professor were seen sitting together.

Note : In case of different persons the articles should be repeated.

This is *a* historical fact.

This is *an* historical fact.

This is quite novel scheme.

This is quite *a* novel scheme.

What fool you are.

What *a* fool you are.

The educated Indians take very little interest in the female education.

Educated Indians take very little interest in the female education.

Note : Educated Indians in general are meant and so 'the' may be omitted.

Those who are not *the* members of this party should leave the room.	Those who are not members of this party should leave the room.
The majority of men who join our college belong to the Hindu community.	The majority of *the* men who join our college belong to the Hindu community.
One thing that I hate in his character is his habit of railing at others.	*The* one thing that I hate in his character is his habit of railing at others.
This letter requires *an early* attention.	This letter requires *early* attention.
The running waters are deepest.	Running waters are the deepest.
In *the case* of fire give alarm.	In *case* of fire give alarm.
Wise are always helpful to the ignorant.	*The* wise are always helpful to *the* ignorant.
Rich should help the poor.	*The* rich should help the poor.
Indians are a great nation.	The Indians are a great nation.
Kalidas is Shakespeare of India.	Kalidas is *the* Shakespeare of India.
Delhi is becoming Paris of India.	Delhi is becoming *the* Paris of India.
Sutlej is in flood.	*The* Sutlej is in flood.
This custom is not prevalent in Deccan, but is common in Punjab.	This custom is not prevalent in *the* Deccan but is common in *the* Punjab.

I have purchased this book from *the* Doaba House.	I have purchased this book from Doaba House.
The Honesty is the best policy:	Honesty is the best policy.
The truth will win over all.	Truth will win over all.
Truth of this statement can be challenged.	*The* truth of this statement can be challenged.
Love of money is natural in man.	*The* love of money is natural in man.
The gold is a precious metal.	Gold is a precious metal.
English were after gold of *the* India.	*The* English were after *the* gold of India.
The people must honour their leaders.	People must honour their leaders.
People of Punjab are not so poor.	The people of *the* Punjab are not so poor.

Note : (*i*) Definite article 'The' is placed before : nouns, which cannot be applied to more than an object; *e.g.* : 'the sun', 'the moon', 'the poles', 'the world', 'the north', 'the Bible', 'the Vedas', 'the Gita', etc.

(*ii*) It is placed before an adjective to show it as a whole class ; as, 'the learned', 'the wise', 'the rich'.

(*iii*) It is placed before the names of nations ; as, 'the Chinese', 'the Indians'.

(*iv*) It is used before the names of rivers ; as, 'the Sutlej', 'the Ganges', before the names of the groups of islands ; as, 'the Andamans', 'the West Indies', before the names of gulfs or oceans; as, 'the Arabian gulf', the 'Indian Ocean', before the ranges of mountains', as, 'The Alps', before the descriptive names of the countries or provinces; as, 'the Deccan', 'the Punjab'.

II. Definite article is omitted before abstract nouns, material nouns, collective nouns, except in certain cases, where some noun is used in restricted and specialised forms, as, 'The gold of America', 'The love of money', 'The people of India'.

The girls leave *the* college at 4 p.m.	The girls leave college at 4 p.m.

Note : Articles are omitted in many phrases made by transitive verb, followed by its objects, when the verb and the object cannot be considered as separate entities.

Mohan shook *the* hands with Ram.	Mohan shook hands with Ram.
This is quite out of *the* place.	This is quite out of place.

Note : The articles are omitted in the preposition of phrases.

He was preparing from *the* head to *the* foot.	He was preparing from head to foot.
His mischief came to *the* light.	His mischief came to light.

Note : When different objects are numbered, the articles are omitted for brevity and emphasis.

He took away *the* tables, *the* chairs, *the* cots from my house.	He took away tables, chairs and cots from my house.
The lovers went hand in *the* hand.	The lovers went hand in hand.

Man to *the* man he was superior to me.	Man to man he was superior to me.
This is *a* news to me.	This is news to me.
Himalayas are highest mountains in world.	The Himalayas are *the* highest mountains in the world.
I heard noise.	I heard *a* noise.
It is quarter to five now.	It is *a* quarter to five now.
I have headache.	I have *a* headache.
I shall stay here for few days.	I shall stay here for *a* few days.
Cloth is sold by yard.	Cloth is sold by *the* yard.
She is in hurry.	She is in *a* hurry.
Hindus are brave people.	*The* Hindus are *a* brave people.
He is *a* M.L.A.	He is *an* M.L.A.
Hindus respect Gita.	*The* Hindus respect *the* Gita.
My brother is player and scholar.	My brother is *a* player and scholar.
A black and *a* white cow is in the field.	A black and white cow is in the field.
He is *the* student of N.D. Victor School.	He is *a* student of N.D. Victor School.
He has obtained *passing* marks in *the* English.	He has obtained *pass* marks in English.
Camel is ship of the desert.	*The* camel is *the* ship of the desert.

Note : 'A' is used before a word beginning with a consonant sound : 'a dog', 'a cow', 'a man', 'a fan'.

He is *an* European.	He is *a* European.

We want *an* university.	We want *a* university.

Note : 'A' is used before any word beginning with 'u' sound pronounced as 'u'—('yoo) as 'a university', 'a European', 'a union', 'a useful pen'. But when 'u' is not pronounced as 'yoo', it is preceded by the 'u' article 'an' ;—'an uncle', 'an urge'.

'A' is also used before 'o' pronounced as 'wa' ; as, 'a one-sided argument', 'a one-eyed man', 'a one-rupee note'.

'A' is again used before a word beginning with an aspirated 'h' as : 'a house', 'a hole' ; use 'an' in place of 'a' where 'h' is silent : as, in, 'an honour', 'an honest man', 'an hout', 'an heir', e.g. ;

I saw him *a* hour ago.	I saw him *an* hour ago.

Note : 'An' is used :

(*i*) Before a vowel as : 'an enemy', 'an inkpot', 'an umbrella', 'an owl', 'an orange'.

(*ii*) Before a word beginning with a silent 'h' as 'an heir', 'an honest man', 'an hour'.

(*iii*) Before a consonant, with sounds like a vowel, *e.g.* : 'an M.A', 'an M.B.B.S', 'an S.P.' and 'an L.L.B'.

He is *a* M.A.	He is *an* M.A.

Note : We use 'a' or 'an' when a proper noun is used in the sense of a common noun, as : 'Kalidas is a Shakespeare of India.' Gandhi is a Socrates of India.'

Note : 'A' is used before a common noun in the singular word to single out an individual as the representation of a class.

Beggar came to me.	*A* beggar came to me.
He is shylock.	He is *a* shylock.

Note : Here shylock is used in the sense of a common noun—'a cruel money lender'.

Note : 'The' is used before the names of 'rivers' 'seas' 'mountains', 'oceans', 'lakes', 'names of seasons' 'directions', 'natural phenomenon', 'newspapers', 'holy books', 'buildings', 'provinces', 'group of islands', 'the sun', 'the moon', 'the earth', 'the sky', 'the games', 'the north', 'the public', 'the world', 'the universe'.

'The' is used before denoting a nationality or a community : 'The English', 'the Indians' : 'The' is used before descriptive use of some countries or states : 'the United States of America', 'the Punjab', 'the Deccan'.

Dog is a faithful animal.	*The* Dog is a faithful animal.

Note : 'The' is used when a singular noun is meant to represent whole class.

Book you mentioned is out of print.	*The* book you mentioned is out of print.

Note : 'The' is used when we speak of a particular person' a thing or one already referrerd to or known to the speaker.

He is ablest speaker of the college.	He is *the* ablest speaker of *the* college.

Note : 'The' is used with the superlatives, because they specify singular objects.

Sooner it is done, better it is.	*The* sooner it is done *the* better it is.

Note : We use 'The' as an adverb with a comparative : 'the more', 'the merrier'.

He is man we like.	He is *the* man we like.
Pen is mightier than sword.	*The* pen is mightier than *the* sword.

Note : 'The' is used before nouns employed in a special sense :

Judge in him revolted.	*The* judge in him revolted.

Note : 'The' here gives an idiomatic meaning of an abstract noun. The judge means—(the spirit of justice). We also use 'The' in fixed idiomatic phrases as : 'in the wrong', 'in the dark', 'put to the test', 'on the contrary', 'to the rescue'.

Note : 'The' article is not used before the following :

(*i*) Before proper nouns, unless they are used as common nouns : 'Bombay', 'Kalidas'.

(*ii*) Before abstract nouns : 'Honesty', 'truth', 'beauty'.

(*iii*) Before names of materials : —'Gold' 'silver,' 'copper'.

(*iv*) Before plural nouns that denote a class : 'poets love nature'.

(*v*) Before names of 'diseases', 'sciences', 'sports', 'things' single in kind :

'Hockey', 'God', 'heaven', 'dancing', 'medicine', 'cholera', 'plague', 'cricket'.

(*vi*) Before the nouns in certain idiomatic phrases : 'Take to 'heart', 'at day break', 'to bring wood', 'at breakfast', 'catch fire', 'by air', 'by sea', 'by name', 'in debt', 'by fair or foul means', 'on horse back' 'to lose heart', 'to set foot', 'to set sail', 'to give ear', 'to take out', 'to take offence', 'on foot', 'ingest', 'by leaps and bounds', 'at dead of night', 'out of reach', 'by dint of', 'by word of mouth', 'to shake hands', 'to leave school', 'to take oath', 'to follow suit', 'to call in mind', 'out of place', 'to live from hand to mouth'.

(*vii*) Before 'times of the year', 'seasons', 'days of week' : 'June', 'Sunday', 'Deepawali'. Collective nouns used in a general sense do not take a definite article as : 'Mankind', 'parliament', 'society', 'cattle', 'posterity'.

(*viii*) Before names of regular meals, names of things single in kind : 'Breakfast', 'dinner', 'lunch', 'hell', 'heaven', 'god'.

(*ix*) Before certain titles, names indicating relationship : 'Emperor Ashoka', 'President Nasser', 'Rai Bahadur'.

(*x*) Before a noun used in its widest sense 'Man is mortal' 'What kind of flower is it?'

(*xi*) Before plural nouns used to denote a class in general sense : 'Lawyers are generally clever'.

We were first to reach there.	We were *the* first to reach there.
What *a* honest woman she is.	What *an* honest woman she is.
Little money is better than none.	*A* little money is better than none.
The both friends went there.	*Both the* friends went there.

He is *in* wrong.	He is in *the* wrong. Or he is wrong.
U.N.O. is international body.	*The* U.N.O. is *an* international body.
I have read whole *the* book.	I have read *the* whole book.
I replied to him in negative.	I replied to him in *the* negative.
Horse is beast of burden.	Horse is *the* beast of burden.
He is out of *the* danger.	He is out of danger.
He is *a* honourable man.	He is *an* honourable man.
Which colour do you like, the blue or brown?	Which colour do you like, the blue or *the* brown?
I want two rupees and half.	I want two rupees and *a* half.
The cricket is game of choice.	Cricket is *a* game of choice.
The History is a different subject.	History is a different subject.

Verbs

He *was* failed.	He failed.

Note : Intransitive Verb cannot be used in the passive voice.

He *tells* that he is going to school.	He *says* that he is going to school.
He *told me* 'go away'.	He *said to me* 'go away'.
I *said to* him the secret.	I *told* him the secret.

Note : 'Say' is used to assert or declare; 'Tell' to inform narrate, or command, speak to utter words; 'say' refers to the words, while 'speaking' to voice.

Will you please *see* my answer paper.	Will you please *look at* my answer paper.
I advised him but he would not *hear* me.	I advised him 'but he would not *listen to* me.
I *hope* you will fail in the examination.	I *fear* you will fail in the examination.

Note : 'Hope' is your expectation with pleasure.

I requested him for a loan but he *denied*.	I requested him for a loan but he *refused*.
The ship was *drowned* in the sea and all *the* crew *sank*.	The ship *sank* in the sea and all *her* crew was *drowned*.
Keep these books on the table.	*Place/put* these books on the table.

Incorrect	Correct
Until I will die, I *shall* never desert you.	Until I die, I *will* never desert you.

Note : 'Will' with the first person denotes determination and 'shall' simple futurity.

Incorrect	Correct
Mohan said that oil *was* lighter than water.	Mohan said that oil *is* lighter than water.

Note : Universal truths are always reported in the present tense.

Incorrect	Correct
I could not *avail* of his offer.	I could not *avail myself* of his offer.
What *is* the data in this case?	What *are* the data in this case?
Try as we *will*, we would not succeed.	Try as we *may*, we would not suceeed.
Mohan as well as you *are* to blame.	Mohan as well as you *is* to blame.
Either you or he *have* taken my money.	Either you or he *has* taken my money.
Neither Sohan nor his sisters is going.	Neither Sohan nor his sisters *are* going.
This subject is hard *to be learnt*.	This subject is hard *to learn*.

Note : After adjectives active, not passive, infinitive should be used.

Incorrect	Correct
Nothing but play and cinema *make* him happy.	Nothing but play and cinema *makes* him happy.
He shouts at me while talking as if I *am* deaf.	He shouts at me while talking as if I *were* deaf.

You speak as if you *don't* know the facts.	You speak as if you *did not* know the facts.

Note : 'As if' and 'as though' are always followed by a past conditional.

We preferred dying rather than *surrendering*.	We preferred dying than *surrender*.
They *seemed* to have been more careful about their studies in those days.	They *seem* to have been more careful about their studies in those days.
Dare *he to do* it?	Dare *he do* it?
I have committed myself to *help* him with money.	I have committed myself to *helping* him with money.
There *was* his father, sons and other persons in the room.	There *were* his father, sons and other persons in the room.
There *are* heaps more of information to be had from him.	There *is* heaps more of information to be had from him.

Note : Words of quantity, like 'heaps' and 'lots', when used for a great number, require a singular Verb unless they are followed by a plural noun. We say : "There *is* lots of sugar", but "lots of students *were* present."

He made me *to do* this work.	He made me *do* this work.
I regard it *a* fun.	I regard it *as a* fun.
Those who *might* have seen the place know how beautiful it is.	Those who *may* have seen the place know how beautiful it is.

I thought that you *may* ave read this note.	I thought that you *might* have read this note.
I would advise *you buy* the same medicine as I have.	I would advise you *to* buy the same medicine as I have *bought*.
He is one of the noblest men that *I ever knew.*	He is one of the noblest men that *I have ever known.*
He no sooner went in than the girl began to speak ill of him.	*No sooner had he gone* in than the girl began to speak ill of him.
There *are* many a student who *do* not know even this.	There *is* many a student who *does* not know even this.
Either he or I *is* to blame.	Either he or I *am* to blame.
He as well as I *am* guilty.	He as well as I *is* guilty.

Note : When the connective is 'as well as' the verb agrees in number and person with the first one.

He abstained from going out in sun lest he *may* get the sun stroke.	He abstained from going out in the sun lest he *should* get the sun stroke.

Note : 'Lest' is followed by a verb with 'should' as its auxiliary.

He asked *had we written our* exercise.	He asked *if we had* (or *whether we had*) *written* our exercise.
Ram *said can he* read this book.	Ram *asked if he could* read that book.

Krishan asked *to* Mohan why *your* father *is* angry.	Krishan asked Mohan why *his* father *was* angry.
He *does not care* for my advice.	He *pays no heed* to what I say.
I do not care *for you.*	I do not care *for what you do.*

Note : 'I do not care for you' properly used means 'I do not like you as a friend.

He *does not care* for his books.	He *does not take care* of his books.
No one cared for the child after his mother died.	*None took care* of the child after his mother died.
He *does not care* for his work.	He *takes no care* for his work.
I did not wait for *he went* out before I arrived.	I did not wait for *he had gone* out before I arrived.
I met a man who was my friend some time ago.	I met a man who *had been* my friend some time ago
He had been studying in the college *since* a long time.	He had been studying in the college *for* a long time.
I went out for *walking* yesterday.	I went out for *a walk* yesterday.
If I *did* this, I shall be fined.	If I *do* this, I shall be fined.
When I *shall go* to Calcutta I shall see the Victoria Memorial,	When I *go* to Calcutta I shall see the Victoria Memorial.

If I *would have* done this, I *would* have done wrong.	If I *had* done this, I *should* have done wrong.
I have *left* rowing.	I have *given up* rowing.
I *left* playing when my friend arrived there.	I *stopped* playing when my friend arrived there.
I had to *leave* my rights and claims.	I had to *abandon* my rights and claims.
If you *leave* the horse's reins, you will fall.	If you *let go* the horse's reins, you will fall.
I should take *your leave.*	I should take *leave of you.*
I went there in the *noon.*	I went there in the *middle of the day.*
After some time he *knew* what he had done.	After sometime he *realized* what he had done.
He should not *cut* jokes in the presence of others.	He should not *make* jokes in the presence of others.
He knows *to* teach you.	He knows *how to* teach you.
He *cut* his pencil.	He *mended* (or *sharpened*) his pencil.
They *cut* the head of the prisoner.	They *cut off* the head of the prisoner.
I *asked* my servant to bring water.	I *told* my servant to bring me water.
I *like* to play chess.	I *should like* to play chess. or I *want* to play chess.
He is *troubling* me unnecessarily.	He is *giving me trouble/treating me badly/bullying me* unnecessarily.
My foot is *paining.*	My foot is *hurting.* I *have a pain in* my foot.

My head (or tooth) is *paining*.	My head is *aching*.
I *have received* a hurt on my arm.	I *have hurt* my arm.
Krishan *gave* a speech on the prize distribution day.	Krishan *made* a speech on the prize distribution day.
Krishan *made* a lecture.	Krishan *gave* a lecture.
He has learnt how to *sit on* a cycle.	He has learnt how to *ride* a cycle.
He could not *get down* from his cycle.	He could not *get off* from his cycle.
Will you take *out* your shoes.	Will you take *off* (or *remove*) your shoes.
He was *putting on* a sweater though it was so hot.	He was *wearing* a sweater though it was so hot.
Standing before a mirror he *wore* a new suit.	Standing before a mirror he *put on* a new suit.

Note : 'Putting on clothes' refers to the act of dressing. Once the act is over, then the clothes are 'worn'.

I cannot *pull on* with my work.	I cannot *manage* my work.
I have *ordered for* a cup of tea.	I have *ordered a* cup of tea.
I have *disposed* my cycle.	I have *disposed of* my cycle.
I always *put* my books in the almirah.	I always *keep* my books in the almirah.
They *respected* me when I arrived there.	They *showed me respect* (or *treated me with respect*) when I arrived there.

I *had a mind* to play the game.	I *intended* to play the game.
I cannot *maintain* my *livelihood.*	I cannot *earn a living* or *get a living.*
He *struck a blow* on my face.	He *struck me* in the face or *hit me* in the face.
I *shot* the wolf but missed.	I *shot at* the wolf but missed. Or I *missed* the wolf.

Note : "I shot the wolf" means that you hit and killed him.

Do not *play* mischiefs in the class.	Do not *make* or *get up to* mischief in the class.
I *went for* playing tennis and enjoyed.	I *went out for* playing tennis and enjoyed myself.
I *stood third* in the province in the competition examination.	I *was third* in the province in the competitive examination.

Note : It is not wrong grammatically but an Englishman would not use it.

Our team *won* the opponents in the match.	Our team *beat* the opponents in the match.
I *lived* with him for a day.	I *stayed* with him for a day.
Sohan *did* no fault and so he should not be blamed.	Sohan *committed* no fault and so he should not be blamed.

I hope he *must* come.	I hope he *will* come or I am sure he will come or he must come.

Note : Error is caused by two alternative idioms being combined.

Udai Singh *found* Udaipur.	Udai Singh *founded* Udaipur.
I *filled water in* the pitcher.	I *filled the pitcher with* water.
Try to *fair out* your written exercise.	Try to *make a fair copy* of your written exercise.
Will you *open* the light.	Will you *turn* the light *on*.
Please *shut* the light.	Please *turn off* the light.
My arm *has been operated.*	On my arm I *have had an operation.*

Note : 'Operate' in the surgical sense must only be used in the active voice followed on :

It is *written* in his letter that . . .	He *says* in his letter that . . .

Note : This is not wrong, but English is clumsy.

I must *revenge* my brother.	I must *avenge* my brother.
I must *avenge* my enemy.	I must *take revenge* on my enemy.

Note : To avenge my brother means 'to punish someone who has hurt my brother.

When your brother comes you must *wish* him.	When your brother comes you must *greet* him or *welcome* him.

In the tennis match I *gave* him a love set.	In the tennis match I *beat* him in a love set or I *took* a love set *off* him.
I *availed* of the opportunity.	I *availed myself* of the opportunity.
Don't *absent from* the classroom.	Don't *absent yourself from* the classroom.

Note : Some verbs take reflexive pronouns after them. Other verbs are 'spread', 'dress', 'hide', 'laid', 'avail', 'disperse' etc. But these can be used without a reflexive pronoun also :

You should not *behave to* bad habits.	You should not *behave yourself to* bad habits.
Let me *bethink of* a suitable way.	Let me *bethink myself* of a suitable way.
I *pride in* this victory.	I *pride myself in* this victory.
Don't *commit to* this way of dealing with him.	Don't *commit yourself to* this way of dealing with him.
I always *interest in* reading books.	I always *interest myself in* reading books.
He should not *overeat* if he wishes to maintain his health.	He should not *overeat himself* if he wishes to maintain his health.
He has grown lazy because he *oversleeps*.	He has grown lazy because he *oversleeps himself*.
He *acquitted* honourably.	He *acquitted himself* honourably.

Never *demean* too much.	Never *demean yourself* too much.
Bid him to do this.	*Bid him* do this.

Note : The sign of infinitive is not used after the verbs : 'bid', 'dare', 'need', 'make', 'see', 'feel', 'hear', 'observe', 'behold' ;

He *need not to* go there.	He *need not* go there.
He *cannot dare to* see me.	He *dare not* see me.
Make the child to sleep.	*Make the child* sleep.
I often hear you *speaking* ill of me.	I often hear you *speak* ill of me.
It is better to sit idle rather *than to work* on this small salary.	It is better to sit idle *than work* on this small salary.

Note : The infinitive without 'to' is also used after 'rather than', 'had rather', 'would rather', 'sooner than', 'had better' etc.

I *would rather die than to* see him.	I *would rather die than* see him.
I *had better take to* leave of you.	I *had better take* leave of you.
Entering the room, the clock struck five.	Entering the room, I heard the clock strike five.

Note : Wrong relation of the participle with the noun.

I saw that the cow *is* let loose.	I saw that the cow *was* let loose.

Note : The sequence of tenses, if the verb in the principal clause is in the past tense, the verb in the dependent clause should be past tense.

2. If the verb in the principal clause is in the present or future tense, the verb in the dependent clauses may be of any tense.

He promised that he *will* send me money.	He promised that he *would* send me money.
The man says that he *would* not do this work.	The man says that he *will* not do this work.
He says that he *could* solve *that* question.	He says that he *can* solve *this* question.
He said that the earth *was* round.	He said that the earth *is* round.
The flood in Sutlej *has worked* a havoc in Ludhiana last year.	The flood in Sutlej *worked* a havoc in Ludhiana last year.
Do you know how this house *took fire.*	Do you know how did this house *take fire.*

Note : Present perfect tense is used in referring to a completed action.

Here is my pitcher; kindly *fill.*	Here is my pitcher; kindly *fill it*.
To whom *you will* speak ?	To whom *will you* speak ?

Note : Mark the question form in the sentence (above). Verb comes after the subject.

Not only the Principal but also the students *were playing.*	Not only the Principal, but also the students *were playing* (or not only the students but also the Principal was playing.)

Note : When two nouns or pronouns are formed by "not only", and "but also", the verb must agree with the second Noun or Pronoun.

Our only guide *were the teachers.*	Our only guide *was the teachers.* (or the *teachers were* our only guide.)

Note : A verb should agree .with its subject and not with the complement.

Bread and butter *are* my food.	Bread and butter *is* my food.
A hue and cry *were* raised.	A hue and cry *was* raised.

Note : When two singular nouns express a single idea the verb is singular.

Many a boys were there.	*Many a boy was* there. Or (*many boys were* there)

Note : "Many a" should always be followed by a singular noun and singular verb. But when "many a" is followed by two nouns of distinct meanings the verb is plural, as : Many a boy and girl were playing.

He *kept himself away* from college.	He *kept away* from college.
The sun has *set itself in* the West.	The sun has *set in* the West.
He *qualified himself as* a teacher.	He *qualified as* a teacher.

Note : In certain words like—'keep', 'dash', 'break', 'more', 'bathe', 'open', 'sat', 'spread', 'turn', 'draw', 'rest', 'well', 'enlist', 'burst', 'gather', 'hide', 'feed', 'qualify', 'form', 'steel', 'stop', 'make', 'repent', 'lengthen'—do not use reflexive pronouns, as : 'myself', 'itself', 'herself', 'himself', etc.

He *resigned to* his fate.	He *resigned himself to* his fate.
He *absented from* his class.	He *absented himself from* his class.
He *avenged upon* his enemies.	He *avenged himself upon* his enemies.

Note : Verbs like—'avail', 'acquit', 'absent', 'avenge', 'distinguish'. 'exert', 'enjoy', 'overeat', 'resign', 'drink', 'oversleep', 'overreach', 'apply', 'set' etc., need a reflexive pronoun after them.

He is *described a* selfish man.	He is *described as a* selfish man.

Note : Verbs like—'define', 'depict', 'mention', 'regard', 'represent', 'treat'—are followed by 'as'.

I *called him as a* fool.	I *called him a* fool.

Note : Verbs like—'elect', 'think', 'call', 'appoint' etc., are not followed by "as".

I *wish it was* over.	I *wish it were* over.
This is *one of the best book* that *has* been published.	This is *one of the best books* that *have* been published.
It is no *use to go* there.	It is no *use going* there.

This book is not *worth to buy.*	This book is not *worth buying.*
I do not want *Mohan going* there.	I do not want *Mohan's going* there.

Note : The noun or pronoun should be put in the possessive case.

The *patient died* before doctor came.	The *patient had died* before the doctor came.

Note : The past perfect is generally used to show certain action or event took place before something else happened.

The *poet and scholar are dead.*	The *poet and scholar is dead.* (or the *poet and the scholar are dead*).
The *carriage and horse are* standing there.	The *carriage and horse is* standing there.

Note : If there is one article or one thing, the verb is singular. If there are two articles or two things, the verb is plural.

Law and order have to be maintained.	*Law and order has* to be maintained.

Note : When two singular nouns have same idea, the verb is singular.

The *Ministry is* divided in the language issue.	The *Ministry are* divided in the language issue.

Note : Here 'ministry' means ministers, so the verb is plural.

The *crowd move* fast.	The *crowd moves* fast.
The *committee have* issued its report.	The *committee has* issued its report.

Note : When a collective noun like—'fleet', 'army', 'committee', 'crowd', is thought as a whole acting together as one unit, it is used in the singular sense.

Two pair of *shoes is* with her.	Two pair of *shoes are* with her.
None but the *brave deserves* the fair.	None but the *brave deserve* the fair.
Our *army has* done well.	Our *army have* done well.

Note : Some nouns like—'number', 'plenty', 'rest', 'variety', 'enemy', 'dozen', 'pair', 'common', 'army',—are plural in meaning though they are singular in form, so the form of verb should be plural.

Sheela as well as her sister *were* present.	Sheela as well as her sister *was* present.
The building with all its furniture *were* sold.	The building with all its furniture *was* sold.
The father together with his sons *are* in the garden.	The father together with his sons *is* in the garden.
Ram as well as Shyam have gone there.	*Ram as well as Shyam has* gone there.

Note: Two nouns connected by 'as well as', 'besides' 'in addition to', 'like', 'with', 'together' are followed by verb in the singular, when the former of the two is in the singular.

Either the brother or the sister *have* done it.	Either the brother or the sister *has* done it.
Either you or I *are* guilty.	Either you or I *am* guilty.
Either I or you *is* at fault.	Either I or you *are* at fault.
Either you or he *are* wrong.	Either you or he *is* wrong.
Either you or your brother *have* broken my slate.	Either you or your brother *has* broken my slate.
Neither the magistrate nor the clerks *was* present.	Neither the magistrate nor the clerks *were* present.
Either he or I *is* guilty.	Either he or I *am* guilty.

Note : Two or more singular nouns or pronouns connected by 'either—or', 'neither—nor', require a singular verb. If the subjects differ in number, or in person, the verb follows the number and person of the subject which stands nearest to it.

Neither of the two girls *were* there.	Neither of the two girls *was* there.

Note : When 'either' or 'neither' are used as nouns or as adjectives, they must have singular verb.

I have never and will never go there.	I have never *gone* and will never go there.

Note : Two auxiliary verbs are used with one principal verb, when the form of the principal verb allows.

Everyone of them *have* a book.	Everyone of them *has* a book.
Each of the four boys *have* gone there.	Each of the four boys *has* gone there.

Note : Singular verb follows 'each', 'every', 'everyone', 'neither', 'either', 'many a'.

A little of good habits *make* our life happy.	A little of good habits *makes* our life happy.
Less than a million of rupees *are* required.	Less than a million of rupees *is* required.

Note : When adjectives like 'much', 'less', 'little', 'more' are used as nouns they must have singular verb.

Neither *he went* there nor *I did.*	Neither *did* he *go* there nor *did I.*

Note : The verb comes before its subject when it is introduced by 'neither' or 'nor', even in case of 'no sooner', 'hardly', the verb comes before the subject.

He told me that he *went* to Simla last month.	He told me that he *had gone* to Simla last month.
If I *was* you, I should not do it.	If I *were* you, I should not do it.
I wish I *was* there.	I wish I *were* there.

Note : In a subjective mood, when there is an expression of some wish or supposition, the verb is plural.

He *will* sit and dream all day.	He *would* sit and dream all day.

Note : 'Will' and 'would' can be used in the sense of habit in all persons, present time being denoted by 'will' and the past time by 'would'.

I have many troubles *to suffer.*	I have many troubles *to suffer from.*
He left for Bombay on Sunday *arriving* there on Tuesday.	He left for Bombay on Sunday *and arrived* there on Tuesday.
I *went for* seeing my brother.	I *went to* see my brother.

Note : The gerund with a preposition must be used instead of the infinite purpose,

He stopped me *to go* there.	He stopped me *from going* there.

Note : We use a gerund and not an Infinive after the verbs—'stop', 'prevent', 'insist', 'succeed', 'hinder', 'persist'.

I enjoy *to walk*	I enjoy *walking.*
This radio is not *worth to buy.*	This radio is not *worth buying.*
He avoids *to go* there.	He avoids *going* there.

Note : Gerund is verbal noun—like 'going', 'buying'. The verbs—'avoid', 'dislike', 'dread', 'enjoy', 'help', 'remember'; 'stop', 'succeed', etc., take gerunds.

Mohan as well as Sohan *are* wrong.	Mohan as well as Sohan *is* wrong.

Note : In sentences, where words are joined to a singular subject by 'as well as', the verb is singular.

Sitting on the gate a wasp hit her.	*While* she was *sitting* on the gate, a wasp hit her.

Note : When a sentence begins with a participle, it qualifies the subject and should agree with a subject. present participle is a verb ending in "ing"—'sitting', 'running' and 'going'.

The committee *is* divided in this question.	The committee *are* divided in this question.
The majority *are* opposed to it.	The majority *is* opposed to it.

Note : Some nouns like—'cabinet', 'crowd', 'committee', 'council', 'jury', 'majority'—are singular or plural accordingly considered collectively or individually.

Waiting for the train a friend came.	*When we were waiting* for the train, a friend came.

Note : The noun is pronoun for which a participle refers in a sentence, should be clearly stated.

We shall no longer cry as we have in the past.	We shall no longer cry as we have *cried* in the past.
A number of writers *has* come.	A number of writers *have* come.

Note : A number of writers 'shows' the idea of plurality.

He *filled water* in the pot.	He *filled the pot* with water.
His tooth is *paining.*	His tooth is *aching.*
The train *stayed* here for five minutes.	The train *stopped* here for five minutes.
I *lived* there for five days.	I *stayed* there for five days.
He *enquired that* where I studied.	He *enquired* where I studied.
I have requested him *do not* befool me.	I have requested him *not to* befool me.
He has not succeeded *to win* the prize.	He has not succeeded *in winning* the prize.
I *have worked* here for the last ten years.	I *have been working* here for the last ten years.
It is up to him *to go or to stay.*	It is up to him *to go or stay.*
You are not selfish, nor *I am.*	You are not selfish, nor *am I.*
None of them *are* of much use in life.	None of them *is* of much use in life.
I cannot *but like* her.	I cannot *help liking* her.
His mother *died since* last Monday.	His mother *has been dead since* last Monday.
She *was put a question.*	*A question was put* to her.
He *ordered* to withdraw *the army.*	He *ordered his army* to withdraw.
How you know her.	*How do you* know her.
He came to me *for seeing* my uncle.	He came to me *to see* my uncle.

Later on *he knew* his mistake.	Later on *he realised* his mistake.
He *was* my Professor five years ago.	He *had been* my Professor five years ago.
The cost of paper and printing *were* too high.	The cost of paper and printing *was* very high.
He *laid* in bed for two hours.	He *lay* in bed for two hours.
He *hurted* his leg.	He *hurt* his leg.
The wood cutter has *fallen* trees.	The wood cutter has *felled* trees.
The enemy has *flown* away.	The enemy has *fled* away.

Note : 'Flow', 'flowed' 'fly', 'flew', 'flown', (for birds) 'flee', 'fled', 'fled'—(for persons).

Adverbs

Incorrect	*Correct*
The child is *very worse* than what you said.	The child is *much worse* than what you said.
The boys left the class *by and by*.	The boys left the class *one by one*.
On seeing his wife he was *very pleased*.	On seeing his wife he was *much pleased*.
It is *much hot* today.	It is *very hot* today.

Note : (*i*) 'Much' is used with adjectives or adverbs in the comparative degree, 'Very' is used with Adjectives or Adverbs in the Positive degree.

(*ii*) 'Much' is used with the past participles, 'Very' is used with the present participles. But this rule is not strictly followed.

(*iii*) 'Very' is used in the sense of really, truly. As such it emphasises the adjectives in the superlative degree.

(*iv*) 'Very' is sometimes used and added to qualify 'much', as : 'This room is *very much* better than that.

Lahore is a *much large* city but a *much* dirty one.	Lahore is a *very large* city but a *very* dirty one.
I was *very annoyed* at his attitude.	I was *much annoyed* at his attitude.
This is a *much* amusing situation.	This is a *very* amusing situation.

Incorrect	Correct
This is the *much best* book on poetry that is available in the market.	This is the *very best* book on poetry that is available in the market.
This mango is *very bad* to be eaten.	This mango is *too bad* to be eaten.
All the water flowed out of the bucket *by and by*.	All the water flowed out of the bucket *little by little*.
You should go *directly* to your father.	You should go *direct* to your father.
He behaved *most gentlemanly*.	He behaved *in a most gentlemanly manner*.
He must do this work whether he will *or not*.	He must do this work whether he will or *no*.
She *exactly stood* in front of me.	She *stood exactly* in front of me.

Note : An adverb generally follows an intransitive verb and the objective of the transitive verb.

Incorrect	Correct
Never *I have* seen such a fool.	Never *have I* seen such a fool.
It is *much harmful* than useful.	It is *more harmful* than useful.
He spoke very *hasty*.	He spoke very *hastily*.
He was *too happy* to meet me.	He was *very happy* to meet me.
Such language sounds *harshly*.	Such language sounds *harsh*.
I am going to the college everyday *since* six years.	I am going to the college everyday *for* the last six years.

Note : 'Since' is used for the point of time from

which the action begins. 'For' is used for the period of time.

Is your mother ill ? *Of course*, she is.	Is your mother ill ? *Yes*, she is.

Note : 'Of course' is used when the thing mentioned is naturally true.

Most *likely* I shall come to see you tomorrow.	Most *probably* I shall come to see you tomorrow.
The boy was *named as* Mohan.	The boy was *named* Mohan.

Note : 'As' is used after the verbs of description only such as 'represent', 'portray', 'mention', 'define', etc.

He did his sum *wrongly*.	He did his sum *wrong*.
The *whole India* feels deeply the loss of its leader.	The *whole of India* feels deeply the loss of its leader.
It is *no one* else *but* me.	It is *none* else *than* I. Or it is *not other* than I.
The mango is *very bad* to be eaten.	The mango is *too bad* to be eaten.
The table is *very* heavy.	The table is *too* heavy.
The sugar is *too* sweet.	The sugar is *very* sweet.
The weather is *too* cold.	The weather is *very* cold.
The weather is *very* cold for me to sit outside.	The weather is *too* cold for me to sit outside.

Note : 'Too' is used where we imply some limit or correct standard. It denotes a kind of excess over the necessary limit or aim. When no limit or standard is implied, we use the adverb 'very' to qualify the adjective.

Long *before* this place was absolutely barren.	Long *ago* this place was absolutely barren.

Note : '*Ago*' is used as an adverb of time. It is never used as a conjunction or preposition.

I was *much* sorry to learn this.	I was *very* sorry to learn this.
I was *much* pleased to see you.	I was *very* pleased to see you.
He was *very* kind enough to write me.	He was *so* kind as to write me, or, he was *kind* enough to write me.
It is nothing else *than* pride.	It is nothing else *but* pride.
Call him anything else *than* a fool.	Call him anything else *but* a fool.

Note : "Else" should be followed by the adverb 'but' in cases noted above.

You are *enough foolish* to go there.	You are *foolish enough* to go there.

Note : The Adverb 'Enough' is generally used after the word it modifies.

I was compelled *to quickly* do this work.	I was compelled to do this work *quickly*.

Note : An adverb should not be used before an infinitive and its size.

He speaks the truth *always*.	He *always* speaks the truth.
She is *wonderful* beautiful.	She is *wonderfully* beautiful.

Note : Adjectives should not be used for adverbs.

He comes to my house *often*.	He *often* comes to my house.
He tells *never* a lie.	He *never* tells a lie.
He goes there *frequently*.	He *frequently* goes there.
He *feels sad* sometimes.	He *sometimes feels* sad.

Note : The adverbs of time—'seldom', 'never', 'ever', 'always', 'often', 'sometimes', 'frequently', etc., are generally used before the verbs they modify.

This news is *very good* to be true.	This news is *too* good to be true.

Note : The adverb 'too' is used in the sense of more than enough but not in that of very much. 'Too' is used also to mean also and as well; as, 'take the boys to the cinema too'.

I am *quite* sorry to hear the sad news.	I am *very* sorry to hear the sad news.

Note : Do not use 'quite' in the sense of 'very' or to a considerable degree.

Does he play well? *Of course*, he does.	Does he play well? *Certainly*, he does.

Note : 'Of course' is often loosely used for 'certainly'.

Firstly you should be regular, and *secondly.* hard-working.	*First* you should be regular and *secondly,* hard-working.

Note : In an enumeration say—'firstly', 'secondly', 'thirdly' etc., *use first* which is an adverb.

I *only worked* two sums.	I *worked only* two sums.

Note : As a rule, the word 'only' should be placed immediately before the word it is intended to modify.

He writes *carefully his* exercises.	He writes *his exercises* carefully.

Note : With a transitive verb the adverb generally comes after the object. If, however, object is long the adverb may come after the transitive verb : —'He writes carefully all the exercises he had to do.'

I *never* remember having met him.	I *do not* remember ever having met him.

Note : The use of 'never' for 'not' is incorrect, for 'never' means 'not ever' and not 'not'.

He had *almost* reached his goal.	He had reached *almost* his goal.
He *eagerly wishes* to help me.	He *wishes eagerly* to help me.
He *fluently spoke.*	He *spoke fluently.*
His grandfather *peacefully died.*	His grandfather *died peacefully.*

Note : When the verb is intransitive, the adverb or the adverbial phrase is placed after the verb. But when the verb is transitive an adverb can be placed either before the verb or after the verb.

I *explained briefly* my idea.	I *briefly explained* my idea or I explained my idea briefly.
He cannot *even write* correct Hindi.	He cannot *write even* correct Hindi.
He *was fortunately* not there.	*Fortunately* he was not there.
I defeated him *at length.*	*At length* I defeated him.

Note : An adverb should be placed at the beginning of a sentence when it is intended to qualify not any word in particular, but the sentence as a whole.

He knows to disgrace others.	He knows *how* to disgrace others.
She worked *nobler* than her sister.	She worked *more nobly* than her sister.

Note : Adjectives should not be used in place of adverbs.

She was walking *much* slowly.	She was walking *very* slowly.
She is *very weaker* than Mohini.	She is *much* weaker than Mohini.

Note : 'Very' modifies adjectives or adverbs in a positive degree and much in the comparative degree.

I am *very* pleased to see you.	I am *very much* pleased to see you.
He is *enough strong* to lift the box.	He is *strong enough* to lift the box.
Urmil is *somewhat* tall for her age.	Urmil is *rather* tall for her age.
The train reached *rather lately.*	The train reached *rather late.*

I found her lying *senselessly*	I found her lying *senseless.*
He recovered his health *by and by.*	He *gradually* recovered his health.
The patient is *very better* today.	The patient is *much better* today.
The luggage is *too much* heavy for me.	The luggage is *much too* heavy for me.
He came *quicker* than I thought.	He came more *quickly* than I thought.
He is *respected greatly.*	He is *greatly respected.*
My heart is *much full* for words.	My heart is *too full* for words.
I saw you *long before.*	I saw you *long ago.*
I have not met him *long since.*	I have not met him *for a long time.*
I did it *presently.*	I did it *just now.*
Your statement is *somewhat* true.	Your statement is *partially* true.
No one *scarcely* goes there.	*Scarcely* anyone goes there.
I could not see him *nowhere.*	I could not see him *anywhere.*

Note: Two negatives destroy each other.

She is *so weak* in English.	She is *very weak* in English.
He is *very weak* that he cannot pass.	He is *so weak* that he cannot pass.

Note: 'So' as an adverb of degree must not be used absolutely without a correlative.

His brother is *very miser.*	His brother is *very miserly.*

He is not so good *like yours*.	He is not so good *as you*.
He sings *very sweet*.	He sings *very sweetly*.
The luggage is *too much heavy* for me.	The luggage is *much too heavy* for me.
Both Dhani and his brother were not present there.	*Neither* Dhani *nor* his brother was present there.
He had scarcely reached his home *than* it began to rain.	He had scarcely reached home *when* it began to rain.
In these days we *scarcely* come across a tiger in jungles.	In these days we *rarely* come across a tiger in jungles.
I finished the work *anyhow*.	I managed to finish the work *somehow*.
I tell you *in brief* I...	I tell you *in short* I...
The train reaches Delhi *soon*.	The train reaches Delhi *quickly*.
Yesterday in the *night*, he came to see me.	Yesterday *evening* he came to see me.
What *for do you* go to his house.	Why *do you* go to his house. Or What *do you* go to his house for.
He sings *good*.	He sings *well*.
Hardly I *have* any rest *since* one month.	Hardly have I *had* any rest for one month.
Really speaking he is not to blame.	*As a matter of fact/To speak the truth/In fact*, he is not to blame.
It is a very interesting book.	It is a very interesting book.
I liked *it on the whole*.	*I liked the whole* of it.

Note : 'On the whole' is only used to sum up. Your opinion of something which is good or bad in parts.

The music in the picture was good though the plot was bad. I liked *the whole of it.*	The music in the picture was good though the plot was bad. I liked it *on the whole.*
She is *quite clever.* She will manage everything.	She is *very clever.* She will manage everything.
Of course Krishan is the most handsome boy in our family.	Krishan is *certainly* the most handsome boy in our family.
Is death inevitable ? *Certainly*, it is.	Is death inevitable ? *Of course*, it is.

Note : 'After all' denotes inspite of what has gone before. It should not be used when we mean some natural consequence. 'Finally' will suit there better.

I *care* a bit for you.	I *do not care* a bit for you.

Special Uses of Some Important Adverbs

Both 'very' and 'much' are used as adjectives and as adverbs : As adjectives they qualify nouns, as :

This is the *very* boy I was looking for.

There was *much* noise in the class.

'Very' is used with adjectives and adverbs in the Positive degree, 'much' in the comparative, as :

He is very old. She is very seriously ill.

He is much older than Prem.

She was much more seriously ill than I thought.

'*Very*' is used with present participle in past participle when used as adjective, 'much' is used with the past participle, when the past participle is a part of the principal verb, as :

He has *very pleasing* manners. I am a very *contented* man. She told a *very interesting* story. I am *much pleased.* He is *much interested* in his work.

Note : In colloquial speech the use of very in such sentences passes as correct; as : 'I am very pleased', 'I am very tired', etc. But it is more correct to use 'much' in such cases.

Since : As an adverb 'since' has mainly two meanings :

(1) 'From then'–I saw him three years ago and have not met him *since.* (or ever since then).

(2) As a conjunction 'since' means '*from which*'. Three years have passed *since* I saw him.

(*ii*) It also means—seeing that

I shall also attend the camp, *since* you wish.

Ago : means past or gone by ; as :

(1) As an adjective it is used after the noun :
I came here a year ago.

(2) As an adverb, it is used in the phrase 'long ago' :
This happened long ago'.

Quite : means completely, perfectly, as :
I am *quite* well.

Of course : means a matter of course or by natural consequence. It does not mean certainly or undoubtedly. He overworked himself and *of course* he fell ill.

By and by : means after an interval or before long. I will tell you about it *by and by*. The use of this phrase in the sense of 'little by little' or 'gradually' is wrong.

Preposition

Incorrect	*Correct*
Send this letter *on* this address.	Send this letter *to* this address.
Do not interfere *in* my work.	Do not interfere *with* my work.
I object *your* remarks.	I object *to* your remarks.
He is blind *of* his defects.	He is blind *to* his defects.
He is blind *in* one eye.	He is blind *of* one eye.
You must attend *your* work.	You must attend *to* your work.
I am angry *with* your rudeness.	I am angry *at* your rudeness.
He is angry *at* me.	He is angry *with* me.
I do not desire *for* a change.	I do not *desire a* change.
I am suffering *with* fever.	I am suffering *from* fever.
He is afraid *from* the dog.	He is afraid *of* the dog.
He is kind *upon* me.	He is kind *to* me.
This is different *to* that.	This is different *from* that.
I was satisfied *by* his work.	I was satisfied *with* his work.
Ram married *with* Sita.	Ram *married* Sita.
The President *called for* a meeting.	The President *called* a meeting.
I signed *on the* agreement.	I signed *the* agreement.

I arrived *to* this conclusion.	I arrived *at* this conclusion.
I met him *in* the way.	I met him *on* the way.
I am sorry *at* his loss.	I am sorry *for* his loss.
Do not knock *the* door.	Do not knock *at the* door.
He was charged *of* theft.	He was charged *with* theft.
He was accused *with* theft.	He was accused *of* theft.
He invited me *at* tea.	He invited me *to* tea.
Do not find fault *in* my work.	Do not find fault *with* my work.
He deprived me *from* my pen.	He deprived me *of* my pen.
I congratulate you *for* your success.	I congratulate you *on* your success.
What is the time *in* your watch.	What is the time *by* your watch.
He is jealous *with* me.	He is jealous *of* me.
Translate this passage *in* English.	Translate this passage *into* English.
I am accustomed *with* cold weather.	I am accustomed *to* cold weather.
He is *in* the committee.	He is *on* the committee.
India does not lack *in* able men.	India does not *lack* able men.
I have no pen *to write*.	I have no pen to *write with*.
He has resigned *from* the post.	He has resigned *the* post.
I arrived *in the* place at exact time.	I arrived at the place *in time*.
He wastes much money *in* trifles.	He wastes much money *on* trifles.

He set the house *to* fire.	He set the house *on* fire.
He does not devote much time *for* studies.	He does not devote much time *to* studies.
There is another side *of* this question.	There is another side *to* this question.
Just *listen me* for a while.	Just listen *to* me for a while.
I do not approve for your conduct.	I do not approve *of* your conduct.
He does not pray God.	He does not pray *to* God.
I have no interest *for* music.	I have no interest *in* music.
He has no taste *in* painting.	He has no taste *for* painting.
He is tired *from* life.	He is tired *of* life.
He was late *for* an hour.	He was late *by* an hour.
He is absorbed *with* his work.	He is absorbed *in* his work.
He climbed *on* the tree.	He climbed *up* (or climbed) the tree.
I told the whole thing *on* his face.	I told the whole thing *to* his face.
He is ashamed *from* his rudeness.	He is ashamed *of* his rudeness.
I have something to ask *from* you.	I have something *to ask* you.
I am indifferent *about* politics.	I am indifferent *to* politics.
Place the lamp *upon* the table.	Place the lamp *on* the table.
He gave me an opportunity *for* reading his letter.	He gave me an opportunity *of* reading his letter.
He is capable *for* doing hard work.	He is capable *of* doing hard work.

He washed his hands *in* water.	He washed his hands *with* water.
His name precedes *before* mine.	His name *precedes mine.*
The jar is full *with* water.	The jar is full *of* water, or is *filled with* water.
I want to get rid *from* him.	I want to get rid *of* him.
We must guard ourselves *from* bad habits.	We must guard ourselves *against* bad habits.
I searched my dog.	I searched *for* my dog.
I waited my father.	I waited *for* my father.
A deputation waited *for* the Prime Minister.	A deputation waited *on* the Prime Minister.
His leg is operated.	His leg is operated *upon.*
He disposed *off* the complaint.	He disposed *of* the complaint.
There is no use *of* acting this.	There is no use *in* acting this.
He was convicted *on the* charge of murder.	He was convicted *of the* charge of murder.
He will be cured *from* fever.	He will be cured *of* fever.
I tried to save him but *of* no purpose.	I tried to save him but *to* no purpose.
She burst *with* tears.	She burst *into* tears.
He died *from* cholera.	He died *of* cholera.
She is quick *in* speech.	She is quick *of* speech.
He *met an* accident.	He *met with* an accident.
He failed *from* four marks.	He failed *by* four marks.
He introduced me *with* his friends.	He introduced me *to* his friends.
I aspire *for the* new post.	I aspire *to the* new post.
Do not quarrel *on* a trifle.	Do not quarrel *over* a trifle.

Diwali corresponds *with* Christmas.	Diwali corresponds *to* Christmas.
I shall explain them this fact.	I shall explain *to* them this fact.
You should contribute something *for* this fund.	You should contribute something *to* this fund.
My brother did not reply me.	My brother did not reply *to* me.
I walked to that place *by* foot.	I walked to that place *on* foot.
She rides *on a* car.	She rides *in a* car.
We saluted *to* him.	We *saluted* him.
He sat *on* a tree.	He sat *in* a tree.
We could not prevail *with* him to go there.	We could not prevail *upon* him to go there.
You must pay *for* your bills.	You must *pay your* bills.
She is ill *from* fever.	She is ill *with* fever.
She was overwhelmed *by* grief.	She was overwhelmed *with* grief.
I have no sympathy *for* him.	I have no sympathy *with* him.
He has been involved *with* serious trouble.	He has been involved *in* serious trouble.
The police will inquire *about* the real cause of trouble.	The police will inquire *into* the real cause of trouble.
How is he related *with* you?	How is he related *to* you ?
She repented *for* her mistake.	She repented *of* her mistake.
I subscribed this magazine.	I subscribed *to* this magazine.
I have no prejudice *for* you.	I have no prejudice *against* you.

He does not fear *from* God.	He does not fear God.
I was late *in* the meeting.	I was late *for* the meeting.
The girl took a fancy *from* this pen.	The girl took a fancy *to* this pen.
She is dominated *with* grief.	She is dominated *by* grief.
This prize is *competed* by all the boys.	This prize is *competed for* by all the boys.
Do not tyranize *on* the poor.	Do not tyranize *over* the poor.
We shall enquire *from* him about it.	We shall enquire *of* him about it.
They came back *in* a few days.	They came back *after* a few days.
I fell *in* the hands of my enemies.	I fell *into* the hands of my enemies.
They are *called with* diffe-rent names.	They are *called by* diffe-rent names.
He boasts *about* his wealth.	He boasts *of* his wealth.
I took the business *into* hand.	I took the business *in* hand.
He complained *of* me to his brother.	He complained *against* me to his brother.
Akbar came *upon* the throne.	Akbar came *to* the throne.
Our examination begins *from* Monday.	Our examination begins *on* Monday.
He did not accede my request.	He did not accede *to* my request.
He did not *comply to* my request.	He did not *comply with* my request.
He came here *on* my invita-tion.	He came here *at* my invitation.

Let us partake *from* this dinner.	Let us partake *of* this dinner.
I caught him *from* the arm.	I caught him *by* the arm.
I regret *at the* delay.	I regret *the* delay.
He rejoiced *on* his success.	He rejoiced *at* his success.
He did not *agree with* my proposal.	He did not *agree to* my proposal.
He did not agree *to* me.	He did not agree *with* me.
He aims *to be* a teacher.	He aims *at becoming* a teacher.
He feels proud *from* his wealth.	He feels proud *of* his wealth.
He takes pride *of* his wealth.	He takes pride *in* his wealth.
The bill was thrown *off*.	The bill was thrown *out*.
Anil is popular *among* his friends.	Anil is popular *with* his friends.
I suspect him *for* stealing the watch.	I suspect him *of* stealing this watch.
The teacher sits *on* his desk.	The teacher sits *at* his desk.
I was surprised *by* her failure.	I was surprised *at* her failure.
Tie the horse *on* a tree.	Tie the horse *to* a tree.
He is trembling *by* cold.	He is trembling *with* cold.
I divided the cake *in* four parts.	I divided the cake *into* four parts.
Do not *add* my worries.	Do not *add to* my worries.
The college term will end *after a* month.	The college term will end *in a* month.
Here is the book *that you asked.*	Here is the book you *asked for*.

I expect a letter from my friend *after* a week.	I expect a letter from my friend *in* a week.

Note: 'After' is used with a period of Past time and not with a period of Future time.

The sun will rise *before* an hour.	The sun will rise *within* an hour.
This is the girl I was *speaking*.	This is the girl I was *speaking of*.
He slept *upto* 4 O'clock.	He slept *till* 4 O'clock.
I walked *till the* end of the street.	I walked *to the* end of the street.

Note: 'Till' is used for time and 'to' is used for place.

The cat is sitting *upon* a table.	The cat is sitting *on a* table.
The cat sprang *on* the table.	The cat sprang *upon* the table.

Note: 'On' is used in speaking of things at rest and 'upon' of things which are in motion.

Note: 'In' and 'at' are used in speaking of things which are at rest or fixed and 'to' and 'into', in speaking of things which are in motion, viz;—'She is in bed.' 'She ran to college.' 'The rat went into the trap'.

Incorrect	*Correct*
What did she *die*?	What did she *die of*?
He is desirous to *go* there.	He is desirous *of going* there.

I am disgusted *of* his habits.	I am disgusted *with* his habits.
I do not have any influence *upon* him.	I do not have any influence *over* him.
She jumped *in* the river.	She jumped *into* the river.
There is a saying *in* the Hindus.	There is a saying *among* the Hindus.
We must act *according to* ideals we hold.	We must act *up to* the ideals we hold.
He has been acquitted *from* the charge.	He has been acquitted *of* the charge.
Accompanied *with his* father he went to Simla.	Accompanied *by his* father he went to Simla.
I beat the dog *by* a stick.	I beat the dog *with* a stick.
You should not grieve *at* the loss.	You should not grieve *over* the loss.
The ceiling fan is *on* my head.	The ceiling fan is *over* my head.
Your hat is similar *with* mine.	Your hat is similar *to* mine.
I passed *near* the Post Office.	I passed *by* the Post Office.
I am not adopted *to* that kind of work.	I am not adopted *for* that kind of work.
I have adopted myself *with* the atmosphere.	I have adopted myself *to* the atmosphere.
I shall be forced to dispense his services.	I shall be forced to dispense with his services.
He attacked *on* Rama with a knife.	He attacked Rama with a knife.
Please credit this sum *in* my name, or in my account.	Please credit this sum *to* my name, or to my account.

Mohan prevented her *to* come here.	Mohan prevented her *from* coming here.
He prohibited his servant *to* his room.	He prohibited his servant *from entering* his room.
There is another side *of* the question.	There is another side *to* the question.
The money given was between six thousand *to* eight thousand.	The money given was between six thousand *and* eight thousand.
Please divide these mangoes *between* these six boys.	Please divide these mangoes *among* these six boys.
Krishan persisted *to say* this.	Krishan persisted *in saying* this.
He meditates his past happenings.	He meditates *upon* his past happenings.
He meditates *upon a* fresh attempt.	He meditates *a* fresh attempt.

Note: 'Meditate', when referring to past takes a preposition but not when referring to future.

I am confident *to win* this match.	I am confident *of winning* this match.
He resigned himself to *failure* in the examination.	He resigned himself to *failing* in the examination.
My attempt to mend him was *in vain*.	My attempt to mend him was *vain*.
He has been deaf *since* his birth.	He has been deaf *from* his birth.
He died *with* hunger.	He died *of* hunger.
He threw a blanket *on* himself.	He threw a blanket *over* himself.

The stone thrown at me fell *in* the ground.	The stone thrown at me fell *to* the ground.
He arrived *to* this conclusion.	He arrived *at* this conclusion.
He asked many questions *to* me.	He asked many questions *from* me.
We lack *in* good students in our college.	We *lack* good students in our college.
A few copies of my testimonials are *attached herewith.*	A few copies of my testimonials are *attached hereto*. (Or: Copies of testimonials are *enclosed.*)
This is my *first time to play* cricket *since* a long time.	This is my *first game* of cricket *for* a long time.
This cloth is inferior *than* that.	This cloth is inferior *to* that.
He wrote me *a letter.*	He wrote *to me.*
I shall *explain him my fault.*	I shall explain *my fault to him.*
He suggested me this point.	He suggested *to me* this point.
There is no harm *to do* this work.	There is no harm *in doing* this work.
Please write this answer *with* ink.	Please write this answer *in* ink.
He rides *on* a tonga.	He rides *in* a tonga.
That is a comfortable house to live.	That is a comfortable house to *live in.*
This is the road to *go on.*	This is the road to *go by.*
He gave me a pistol *to shoot.*	He gave me a pistol to *shoot with.*
I gave him a chair to *sit.*	I gave him a chair to *sit on.*

They are spending much money *for* luxuries.	They are spending much money *on* luxuries.
He has gone *for doing* some business.	He has gone *in* business.
Mohan went *for riding.*	Mohan went *for a ride.*
When the book was searched it was found.	When the book was searched *for it* was found.
I shall inform my father *about* this.	I shall inform by father *of* this.
Due to headache I cannot go to my office.	*Owing to* headache I cannot go to my office.
The cinema is *on the back side* of my house.	The cinema *is behind* my house, or *on the back of* my house.
They walked fifty miles *by* foot.	They walked fifty miles *on* foot.
The government should compensate the loss.	The government should compensate *for the* loss.
I must go, there is no help.	I must go, there is no *help for* it.
I met *with* your father yesterday.	I met your father yesterday.
This work was done *during* 1920-1922.	This work was done *between* 1920-22.
India grew prosperous *between* Asoka's reign.	India grew prosperous *during* Asoka's reign.
The Punjab is *to* the west of India.	The Punjab is *in* the west of India.
Burma is *in the* east of India.	Burma is *to the* east of India.

Note: 'The Punjab' being a part of India, so 'in'

should be used. 'Burma' being outside India, 'to' should be used.

I went to the college *at* morning.	I went to the college *in the* morning.
I returned from there *in the* noon.	I returned from there *at* noon.
It was *in the* midnight that I woke up.	It was *at* midnight that I woke up.
We go home *at* the evening.	We go home *in* the evening.
I will return *within* an hour.	I will return *in* an hour.
Try to finish this work *in* an hour.	Try to finish this work *within* an hour.
The two brothers shared *amongst* them the property.	The two brothers shared *between* them the property.
The pen is lying *besides* the inkpot.	The pen is lying *beside* the inkpot.
He was *beside* himself with joy.	He was *besides* himself with joy.
Beside this, I have to do other work also.	*Besides* this, I have to do other work also.
Distribute these fruit *between* all these boys	Distribute these fruits *amongst* all these boys.

Note: *'Between' and 'among'* : 'Between' is used for two things and 'among' for more than two.

'In' and 'within' : 'In' means after the lapse of the appointed time, 'within' means before the end of it (appointed time).

'At' and 'in': When these prepositions are used to denote time space, 'at' refers to a small extent, and 'in' to a wider, a larger one.

'Into' and 'in': 'In' signifies motion or rest in a place, 'into' shows motion from one place to another.

'With' and 'by': 'With' denotes the instrument with which a thing is done, and 'by' denotes the agent or the doer.

Your fault admits *no* excuse.	Your fault admits *of* no excuse.
He wastes much money *in* trifles.	He wastes much money *on* trifles.
He does not devote much time *for* studies.	He does not devote much time *to* studies.
He got down *from the* morning train.	He got down *the* morning train.
I arrived *to* this conclusion.	I arrived *at this* conclusion.
Just listen me for a while.	Just listen *to* me for a while.
He is blind *of* his defects.	He is blind *to* his defects.
He is blind *in* one eye.	He is blind *of* one eye.
He is kind *upon* me.	He is kind *to* me.
I have something to ask *from* you.	I have something to *ask you.*
He deals *with* sugar.	He deals *in* sugar.
I regret *at the* delay.	I regret *the* delay.
I got *down from* my bicycle.	I got *off* my bicycle.
He wants to pick *up* a quarrel with everyone.	He wants to pick a quarrel with everyone.
We faced *with* our enemy.	We faced our enemy.
He will be cured *from* fever.	He will be cured *of* fever.
He has been operated *from* cancer.	He has been operated *upon* cancer.
He walked *with* a speed of five miles per hour.	He walked *at* a speed of five miles per hour.

Be careful to guard *from* danger.	Be careful to guard *against* danger.
Don't knock my door.	Don't knock *at* my door.
He is keen *to go* there.	He is keen *on going* there.
He is desirous *to go* there.	He is desirous *of going* there.
He is entitled for vote.	He is entitled *to* vote.
He has no money *with* him.	He has no money *on* him, or *about* him.
I do not have any influence *upon* him.	I do not have any influence *over* him.
She reported *for her* mistake.	She reported *of her* mistake.
This cloth will *wear off* soon.	This cloth will *wear out* soon.
I have no sympathy *for* him.	I have no sympathy *with* him.
I aspire *for* the new post.	I aspire *to* the new post.
Conversation was carried on *by* whispers.	Conversation was carried on *in* whispers.
She is quick *in* speech.	She is quick *of* speech.
She takes pride *in* her beauty.	She takes pride *of* her beauty.
I am confident *to win* the prize.	I am confident *of winning* the prize.
My plan has *fallen.*	My plan has *fallen through.*
I have again encountered *with his* enemy.	I have again encountered *his* enemy.
I avenged myself *against* him.	I avenged myself *on* him.
I am fortunate *to have* such a good brother.	I am fortunate *in having* such a good brother.

Open your book *on* page 65.	Open your book *at* page 65.
It has been raining *from* three hours.	It has been raining *for* three hours.
It has been raining *from* 4 O'clock.	It has been raining *since* 4 O'clock.
Death is preferable *than* dishonour.	Death is preferable *to* dishonour.
I do not believe him.	I do not believe *in* him.
I cannot agree *to* you with this proposal.	I do not agree *with* you (on this point), or to this proposal.

Note: We agree *with* a person, *to* a proposal *on* a point.

Note: There are a few important rules about prepositions which should be kept in view.

Words that do not take Preposition after them.

He ordered my dismissal.	(not ordered for)
He criticised my article.	(not criticised upon)
He regained his money.	(not regained from)
He is spent with toil.	(not spent up)
He obeys my orders.	(not obeys to)
This table resembles that.	(not resembles to)
I will inform my sister.	(not inform to)
Have you signed the papers.	(not signed to or upon)
I have opened a school.	(not opened up)
He ascended the hill.	(not ascended on)
I recommended him.	(not recommended for)

I confused two different things.	(not confused up)
I assisted him in this task.	(not assisted to)
The medicine has benefited me.	(not benefited to)
I carefully investigated the case.	(not investigated with)
You should not violate the rule.	(not violate against)

Note: There are many other such words which do not take Prepositions, and so should be noted carefully by the study of other sentences.

Words where the prepositions are wrongly omitted.

A few are given below. Find out others from study of other sentences.

Depend in his promise.	(not depended his promise)
We are beware of dogs.	(not beware dogs)
Aware of a fact.	(not aware a fact)
Partake of a meal.	(not partake a meal)
Dispose of a work.	(not dispose a work)
Listen to a speech.	(not listen a speech)
Apply to a person.	(not applied a person)
Muse over a matter.	(not muse a matter)

Note: Make a list of such words after study.

In certain words gerund or some equivalent verbal noun should be substituted instead of Infinitive and

made the object to the preposition. A few examples are given below. Find out others :

Addicted to changing.	(not to change)
Aim at preserving.	(not to preserve)
Disqualified for working	(not to work)
Desist from talking.	(not to talk)
Negligent in paying.	(not to pay)
Insist on reading.	(not to read)
Intent on going.	(not to go)
Right in holding.	(not to hold)
Hope of being accepted.	(not to be accepted)
Gift of attracting.	(not to attract)
Fortunate in having.	(not to have)
Fondness for reading.	(not to read)
Excuse for being late.	(not excuse to be late)
Excels in speaking English.	(not excels to speak)
Assisted in doing.	(not assisted to do)
Abstain from speaking.	(not abstain to speak)
Averse to employing.	(not averse to employ)
Bent on coming.	(not bent to come)
Confident of succeeding.	(not confident to succeed—not chance to succeed)
Custom of rising early.	(custom to rise early)
Despaired of success.	(not despaired to succeed)
Discouraged against learning.	(not discouraged to learn)
Dissuade from going.	(Not dissuade to go)
Fearful for failing.	(Not fearful to fail)
Necessity of or for deciding.	(not necessity to decide)
He repented of speaking.	(not repented to speak)

He refrained from speaking.	(not refrained to speak)
Persisted in saying.	(not persisted to say)
Persevered in going.	(not persevered to go)
Passion for studying.	(not passion to study)
Pretext for staying.	(not pretext to stay)
Insisted in his going.	(not insisted to go away)
Prevented from working.	(not prevented to work)
Debarred from completing.	(not debarred to complete)
Prohibited from going.	(not prohibited to go)
Hindered me from doing something.	(not hindered me to do something)

Note: In some cases both Infinitive and Verbal Noun can be used after the 'very'. Note the following examples. Find out others as :
Accustomed *to* walk or, accustomed *to* walking, afraid to *go* or, *afraid of going*, decide *to stay* or, *decide upon staying*.

Note: All verbs followed by a verbal noun ending in 'ing' take 'from' after them except 'forbid' and are used in the sense prevention.

Verbs that take 'in' after them and not 'into'.

To fall *in* line, to come *in* light, to take *in* hand, dipped *in* water, steeped *in* poverty, immersed *in* pleasure, bathed *in* blood, involved *in* difficulty, implicated *in* crime, sink *in* depression, enlist *in* the army, inspired *in* our hearts, engaged *in* business.

Other words that take 'in' after them

Defective *in* body, deficient *in* learning, deformed *in* limbs, experience *in* teaching, firm *in* opinion, failed *in* attempt, fruitful *in* attempt, honest *in* dealing, base *in* morals, obstinate *in* disposition, polite *in* manners, temperate *in* food, profuse *in* apologies, scothful *in* business, abound *in* or *with* living things, abound *in* experience, absorbed *in* thought, acquesce *in* decision, backward *in* learning, believed *in* his word, bound *in* honour, or bound *by* every tie, agree *in* an opinion, or *with* a person, confirmed *in* appointment, confide *in* a person, confide a secret *to* a person, delight *in* his company, disappointed *in* a thing, disappointed *of* a thing (not included in the list), happen *in* a place (at a time, to a person) enveloped *in* a fog, excel *in* drawing, expensive *in* dress, exult *in* success, remiss *in* duty, rich *in* cattle, succeed *in* attempt, versed *in* logic, trust *in* a person, *to* a thing, involved *in* a disgrace, negligent *in* attendance, officiate *in* a post, persevere *in* study, persist *in* a course, taste *in* pictures (judgement) taste *for* anything (Music or Cinema) taste *of* anything (poetry), wanting *in* courage.

Words that take 'into' after them instead of 'in'

Falling *into* passion, burst *into* tears, coming *into* the mind, coming *into* a person's presence, taking *into* consideration, prying *into* a matter, introduce *into* society, plunged *into* a debt, come *into* collisions, sinking *into* insignificance, imported *into* a country, come *into* contact with a person.

Words that take 'of' and not 'in'

Blind *of* an eye, dull *of* hearing, easy *of* access, infirm *of* purpose, lame *of* one leg, lavish *of* expenditure, subversive *of* discipline, forgetful *of* duty, slow *of* speech, sound *of* limb, envious *of* fame, jealous *of* his fame, abhorence *of* deceit, accuse *of* a crime, acceptance *of* a favour, admonished *of* a fault, (and by a person), afraid *of*, ambitious *of* glory, answer *of* a person, to your name for his neglect. apprise *of* his loss, approve *of* his conduct.

Words that take 'with', and not 'by'

Adorned *with* jewels.
Beset *with* difficulties.
Delighted *with* prospect.
Drenched *with* rain.
Fined *with* zeal.
Inflated *with* pride.
Inspired *with* hope.
Overcome *with* fatigue.
Sinitton *with* grief.
Touched *with* pity.
Indignant *with* the fellow.
Disgusted *with* the speaker.
Afflicted *with* lameness.
Contented *with* a little.
Distracted *with* power.
Endowed *with* talent.
Infested *with* rats.
Infused *with* zeal.
Menaced *with* attack.
Provided with money.
Stained *with* views.
Transported *with* joy.
Delighted *with* the gift.
Perish *with* hunger and by the sword.

Cognate *with*, coincide *with*, compatible *with*, identical *with*, synonymous *with*, connect *with* (a person in a trouble).

Words that take 'to' and not 'with'

Acceptable *to*, accommodate oneself *to* circumstances, alternative *to*, appropriate *to*, common *to* both, congenial *to*, indulgent *to*, peculiar *to* the case, proportionate *to* the amount.

Words that take 'upon' or 'on' and not 'for' or 'over'

Congratulate one *upon* one's success, decide *upon* a course of action, determine *upon* going, embark *upon* an enterprise, fix *upon* a day, incumbent *upon* him, resolve *upon* fighting, urge *upon* his consideration, dawn *upon* me, discourse *upon* a proposal, dilate *upon* his plans, effect *upon* his health, encroach *upon* my rights, enlarge *upon* his topic, reflect *upon* the past, meditate *upon* his life, bestowed *upon* the poor, confer *upon* the applicant, consequent *upon* an event, contingent *upon* success, enjoin *upon* officer, entail *upon* childern.

Words that take 'over', and not 'upon'

Control *over* my action, muse *over* old friendship, ponder *over*, tyrannise *over*.

Similar words taking different prepositions

Dependent *on* her.	Independent *of*.
He has a dislike *to* him.	Liking *for* him.
I am sensible *of* pain.	I am insensible *to*.
He is equal *to* me.	He is coequal *with* me.
He is qualified *to* compete.	He is disqualified *from* competing.
My trust *in* you is great.	My distrust *of* you is great.
He encouraged me *to* proceed.	He discouraged me *from* proceeding.

Subsequent *to* his departure.	Consequent *upon* his departure.
I am different *from* you.	Indifferent *to* me.
Neglectful *of* business.	Negligent *in* his business.
According *to*.	In accordance *with*.
Affection *for*.	Affectionate *to*.
Alternate *with*.	Alternative *to*.
Ambitious *for*.	Ambitious *of*.
Alien *to*.	Alienate *from*.
Capable *of*.	Capacity *for*.
Cautious *of*.	Caution *against*.
Confident *of*.	Confidence *in*.
Delight *in*.	Delighted *with*.
Descend *from*.	Descendant *of*.

Desire *for*, desirous *of*; envy *at*, envious *of*; exclude *from*, exclusive *of*; fond *of*, fondness *for*; hinder *from*, hindrence *to*, hope *for*, hope (noun) *of*; prepare *for*, preparatory *to*; sympathy *for*, sympathise *with*; want *of*, wanting *in*.

Words that take more than one prepositions on different occasions.

A letter is directed *to* a person, but a criticism is directed *against* him.

He is vexed *with* a person but is vexed *at* a thing.

Disappointed *of* a thing. (in failing to get it)	Disappointed *in* a thing. (after getting it)
Fail *in* an attempt.	Fail *of* a purpose.

Disgusted *with* a person, *at* a thing.

Angry *with* a person *at* a thing.

Displeased, enraged, annoyed, offended, delighted *with* a person, but *at* a thing. Similarly, we are irritated, provoked, excited, affected *by* persons and *at* events.

The following examples may be noted :

To have the advantage *of* a person, but gain an advantage *over* him.

To agree *with* a person, but agree *to* his proposal.

Accorded *to*—Bad treatment was accorded *to* me.

Accorded *with*—The statements did not accord *with* the truth.

Afflicted *with*—I am afflicted *with* influenza.

Afflicted *at*—I am afflicted *at* your misery

Anxious *for*—He is anxious *for* the prize.

Anxious *about*—He is anxious *about* his health.

Attend *at*—I attended *at* that time.

Attend *to*—I attended in the meeting *to* only one thing.

Begin *at*—Begin your book *at* page 50.

Begin *with*—Begin *with* the first ten pages.

Beg *of*—The culprit begged mercy *of* the judge.

Beg *for*—He begged the judge *for* mercy.

Blush *at*—She blushed *at* the praise of her beauty.

Blush *for*—You need not blush *for* me (conduct).

Bound *for*—I am bound *for* Bombay.

Bound *in*—He is bound *in* honour not to divulge the secret.

Care *of*—Take care *of* your health.

Care *for*—He does not care *for* her.

Concur with }
Concur in } He concurred *with* him in the decision.

Confide in } I confide *in* you.
Confide to } I confide my plans *to* you.

Confident *of*—He is confident *of* his success.

Confident *in*—He is confident *in* the justice of his course.

Cause *of*—What is the cause *of* delay.

Cause *for*—There is no cause *for* delay.

Compare *with*—He compared Napoleon *with* Henry VIII.

Compare *to*—We compare anger *to* fire, world *to* a stage.

Note: Similar things are compared *with* and dissimilar things are compared *to* each other.

Die *of*—People die *of* hunger (of a disease).

Die *by*—Man dies *by* the sword (by violence).

Entrust *with*—I cannot *entrust* anyone *with* this secret.

Entrust *to*—I cannot *entrust* this secret *to* anyone.

Exult *in*—He *exulted in* the misfortune of Rama.

Exult *over*—He *exulted over* his defeated enemy.

Familiar *with*—I am *familiar with* the name of Kalidas.

Familiar *to*—The name of Kalidas is *familiar to* me.

Impatient *of*—He is *impatient of* reproof.

Impatient *for*—I am *impatient for* going to Delhi.

Liable *to*—All people are *liable to* error.

Liable *for*—Who is to be *liable for* payment.

Part *with*—It is difficult to *part with* the friend I love.

Part *from*—I cannot *part from* the series of my early life.

Provide *for*—The mess manager will *provide for* our wants.

Provide *against*—We must *provide against* the risk.

Prevailed *on*—He *prevailed on* me for accompany.

Prevailed *with*—He *prevailed with* me to accept his present.

Prevailed over or against — He *prevailed over* or *against* his enemies.

Reconciled *with*—I am *reconciled with* his brother.

Reconciled *to*—I am *reconciled to* my marriage.

Result *of*—What is the *result of* the negotiations.
Result *from*—Success *results from* a life of purity.
Search *of*—I am in *search of* a job.
Search *for*—He made a *search for* his lost watch.
Slow *of*—He is *slow of* learning.
Slow *at*—He is *slow at* geography.
Succeed *to*—He *succeeded to* his fathers' property.
Succeed *in*—He *succeeded in* his efforts.
Sympathise *with*, *in*—I *sympathise with* you, *in* your misfortune.
Taste *of*—He has had a *taste of* illness.
Taste *for*—He has no *taste for* music.
Tired of—I am *tired of* this sort of life.
Tired with—I am *tired with* the exertion.
Use of—What is the *use of* asking
Use in—There is no *use in* asking.
Use for—I have no *use for* this.
Trust in—*Trust in* God and do the right.
Trust to—I cannot *trust to* my memory.
Trust with—I cannot *trust* you *with* money.
Vengeance upon—He took *vengeance upon* his enemy.
Vengeance for—He took *vengeance for* the wrong inflicted upon him.
War upon—He made *war upon* luxury.
War with—He made *war with* his enemy.

The usage of different prepositions

Accompanied *by* a friend; *in* an expedition.
Adapted to a thing; *adapting for* a purpose.
Advantage of his absence; *advantage over* his opponent.
Affinity with a person or thing; *affinity between* the two.
Agree among themselves; *to* a proposal; *with* a person.
Alight from the horse; *on* the ground; *at* a certain hour.

Allied to a thing; *with* a person.
Angry at a thing; *with* a person.
Annoyed at a thing; *with* a person.
Answer of a person; *to* his name; *for* his neglect.
Ask for a thing; *ask of* a person.
Atone to a person; *for* a fault.
Attendance at court; *upon* a person; *attentive to* teacher.
Beg of a person; *for* bread.
Betray to the enemy; *into* his hands.
Call upon or *on* a person; *at* the office; *for* the parcel.
Compete with a person; *for* a prize.
Complain of a person or a thing; *about* a person or a thing.
Complain to a person; *against* a person.
Concerned at or *about* an event; *for* his safety; *in* the crime.
Confer with a person; *about* a thing; *confer* a favour on a person.
Consist of metal; *in* causes or results.
Contend with or *against* a person; *for* or *about* a thing.
Converse with a person; *on* a subject.
Correspond with a person; *about* a subject; *to* an object.
Deal with a person; *in* a commodity.
Differ with a person; *on* a subject; *in* opitmous.
Eager for a thing; *in* its pursuit.
Enter upon a course; *into* one's plans.
Exception to a rule; *against* a person.
Fail in one's purpose; *fail of* success.
Fall under suspicion; *from* the roof; *into* error; *on* or *upon* an enemy; *in* love; *in* with a proposal; *among* thieves.
Feed in grass (intransitive); *feed with* corn (transitive).
Glance at an objeet; *glance over* a page.
Grieve at an event; *for* a person.

Influence with or over; *on* his conduct.
Inform a person of a thing; *against* a person.
Intrude upon a person; *into* your command into a room.
Invest with authority; *in* land or Bank.
Liable to abuse; *for* the loss.
Moved at the sight; *by* the passion; *to* tear with envy.
Necessary of the case; *for* his going.
Pass by a spot; *over* a fault.
Play at cricket; *on* the harp.
Polite in his manner; *to* all.
Regard for a person; *to* our neighbour.
Rejoice at a thing; *with* a person.
Respect for a person; *of* a matter.
Serviceable to a person; *for* a purpose.
Smile at his folly; *upon* his proposal.
Suitable for the purpose; *to* the occasion.
Triumph over an enemy; *in* a cause.
Unite with a person; *in* an effort.
Wait upon (attend) a person; *wait for* (stay).
Watch for the morning; *over* a person.
Zeal for religion; *against* wrong.

In some cases more than one preposition is used after the same word without altering the meaning.

Ambitious of/for renown; advance upon/against enemy; anology to/with a thing; correspond to/with this; borrow of/from a neighbour; buy of/from a dealer; contend with/against a person; endeavour for/after a success; fight with/against the foe, Ill of/with fever; lenient to/with an offender; moved by/with pity; proposition to/with an amount; provide for/against difficulties; recover from/of a disease; relieved of/from a burden; sympathy for/with him.

Nouns, verbs, adjectives, etc., with the prepositions they generally take after them :

A

Antidote *against*; antipathy *to*; appoint *to* a situation; apprehensive *of* danger; appropriate *to* occasion, ascribe *to* him; approve *of* his conduct; arrive *at* a place; assent *to* a proposal; associate *with*; astonished *at* impudence, atone *to* a person; averse *to* a thing; aware *of* his attention; apart *from*; apprise *of* his loss; ashamed *of* his conduct; ask *for* a thing; assure him *of* safety; avail oneself *of*.

B

Backward *in* learning; banish *from* country; bear *with* a person; bare *of* clothes; bent *on* going; beg *of* a person; bestow a thing *on*; bereaved *of* his wife; boast *of* skill; betray to enemy; borrow *of* or *from* a friend, bathe *in* water; belong *to* a person; beset *with* danger; blame *for* failure.

C

Capable *of* an action; capacity *for* thought; care *for* his life; care *of* his books; caution *against* a thing; cautious *of* fire; cede to Germany; celebrated *for* bravery; charge him *with*; charge him the cost (without preposition) or charge him *for*; cleanse *from* sin; clean *of* debt; close *with* the offer; coincide *with* his opinion; commit *to* memory; committed *against* laws; compatible *with* safety; compensate *for*; compete *with* a person; comply with a request; conceal *from* view; condole *with* a person: comfortable *to* rule; confront *with*; congratulate *on*; connect *with* what goes before; consent *to* the plan; consequent *upon* the proceedings; consult *with* your father; contrary *to* his order; convince *of* error; copy *from* a book; cure one *of* disease; catch *at* a straw; Cavil *at* a speech; certain *of* success; cheat one *of*; close *to* the river; combine *with* enemy; common *to*; competent *for*; composed *of* metal; conduce *to* health; confined *to* bed; congenial *to* taste; connive at crime; consistent *with* a statement; conversant *with*; comment *on* or *upon* an event.

D

Deaf *to* advice; defraud *one of* his dues; demand *of* a person; derived *from*; derogate *from* one's reputation; descriptive *of* the places; deserving *of* praise; desirous *of* gain; desist *from* the chase; destitute *of* food; destructive *of* happiness; detract *from* his good name; die *of* hunger; devolve *upon* or *on* a person; difficulty *in*; diminution *of* comfort; disagree *with*; dislike *to* labour; discouragement *to* virtue; displeased *with* his servant; dispute *with*; distinct *from* the other; distrustful *of* courage; due to want *of* care; decide *on* or *upon* a plan; demur *to* the charge; derogatory to one's good name; designed for use; despair *of* success; determine *upon*; diligent in business; discharge *from*; discourage *from* an attempt; dispense *with* his help; dissent *from* an opinion; doubt *of* one's honesty.

E

Eager *for* a thing; effective *for* war; elicit *from*; embittered *against* a person; emboldened *by* success; envious *of* fame; enamoured *of* a person; encroach *on* or *upon*; endeared *to* a person; endowed *with* beauty; endowed *with*; enjoin *upon* a person; enlarge *upon* a subject; enter *upon* a course; enter *into* one's plans; enveloped *in* fog; envy *at* or envious *of* his success; escape *from* jail; essential *to* health; exact *from* a person; except me *from* payment; exclude *from* society; exclusion *of* anything; exempt *from* duty; expel *from* school; expostulate *with* a person; extricate *from* a difficulty, easy *of* approach; eligible *for* office; eminent *for* skill; encouragement *to* virtue; endeavour *after* a thing; engraved *on* brass; enlist *in* the army; entitled *to* a seat; equal *to*; estimated at; exchange *with*; excuse *for* absence; exposed *to* danger.

F

Favourable *to* his wishes; favoured *with* your company; feel *for* the poor; fertile *in* resource; finish *with* song; fit *for* a purpose; forgetful *of* duty; free *from* blame; full *of* sorrow; familiar *with* the object; fawn *upon* a person; find *out* the cause; foreign *to* purpose; frown *upon* a person.

G

Grasp *at* show; gifted *with* skill; grumble *at* the charge; grateful *to* a person; guard *against* or *from*; glad *of*, *at* the result; greedy *of*; *after* riches; guilty *of*.

H

Healed *of* his disease; hide *from* a person; hope *for* better times; hurtful *to* anything; hurt *at* the cause; hush *up* the tale.

I

Ignorant *of* a subject; ill *of* fever; immersed *in* pleasure; impatient *of* control; impertinent *to* his teacher; impose *upon* a person; impute blame *to* a person; incentive *to* labour; included *in* the list; inclusive *of all* charges; indebted *to* a person; indebted *in* a large sum; indifferent *to* fame; indignant *at* the insult; infer *from*; infringe *on* the rights; introduce *to* a person; introduced *into* a thing; innured *to* hardship; inveigh *against* crime; irrelevant *to* question; irrespective *of* the result; illustrative *of* the subject; impelled *by* pride; impress a thing *upon*; inclined *to* idleness; inculcate *upon* a person; indicative of displeasure; indulgent *to* his children; initiate *into* crime; insist *upon*; intrude *upon* a person; intimate *with*; invite to marriage.

J

Jealous *of* his rights; join *with* a person; judge *of* a person *by* his action.

K

Know *of* anything.

L

Lame *of* a leg; lament *for* his only son; lough *at* him for his folly; lavish *of* money; lost *to* a sense of shame.

M

Made *of* wood; *for* a purpose; marry *to*; martyr *for* a cause; martyr *to* a disease; meddle *with* the watch; meditate *upon* question; meet *with* refusal; militate *against* an opinion; mindful *of* promise; moved *at* sight; mourn *for* a person.

N

Natural *to* a boy.

O

Object *to* a demand; obliged *to* him for a gift; observance *of* the sabbath; occur *to* a person; odious *to* a person; offend *against* a rule; open *to* objection; opposed *to* fact; overcome *with* sleep; overwhelmed *with* joy.

P

Parallel *to* the first; partake *of* food; partial *to* his friend; passion *for* gambling; peculiar *to* the country; penitent *for* his conduct; persevere *in* study; pertain *to* a subject; pray *for* blessing; precious *to* the owner; preferable to the first; prefixed *to* the paper; prejudice against a person; prepare *for* the worst; prepare *against* the idea; presume *upon* his good nature; pretext *for* absence; prevent *from* coming; previous *to* his death; profit *by* transaction; profitable *to* the owner; prohibit *from* giving; prone *to* deceit; proper *for* the occasion; protest *against* the course; proud *of* his position; put *up* with abuse.

Q

Qualified *for* office; quarrel *with* a person; quick *at* accounts.

R

Rebel against the king; recede from his position; reckless of danger; recken *on* profit; recover *from* fever; reduce *to* a state; refer *to* his letter; reign *over* a country; relation *to* a matter; relating *with* a person; relieve *from* the task; relish *for* work; rely *on* or *upon* promise; remind one *of* promise; remit *to*; remote *from* home; repent *of* a deed; repine *at* misfortune; replete *with* luxury; reply *to* a letter; reproach him *for* a fault; require *of* a person; rescue *from* danger; resigned *to* his lot; resolve *upon* a course; resort *to* trickery; respond *to* an appeal; restore *to* an office; revert *to* the owner; rid *of* the whole affair; rob the person *of* a thing; rule *over* the country.

S

Sacred *to* the memory; sanguine *of* success; search *for* or *after* anything; secure *from* or *against*: sensible *of* kindness; sensitive *to* ridicule; shoot *at* a mark; short *of* money; sick *of* idleness; side *with* a person; significant *of* his designs; similar *to* others; snatch *at* the chance; solicitors *of* employment; sorry *for* the loss; sparing *of* praise; specific *for* or *against* a disease; spite *against*; stained *with* sin; sport *with* danger; subject *to* orders; stare *at* a person; strip *off* clothes; subsist *upon* bread; subscribe *to* a fund; subsequent *to* an event; sure *of* success; surprise *at* failure; suspicious *of* danger; swerve *from* the right; sympathise *with* a person; sympathy *for* the poor.

T

Temper *with* the accounts; taste *of* anything; temperate *in* eating; Tempt *with* money; thirst *for* or *after* gain; trample *upon*; trifle *with* the truth; true *to* nature.

U

Urge *upon* a person.

V

Vain *of* his beauty; victorious *over* enemy; vie *with* a person; void of learning.

W

Weary *of* life; wink *at* his neglect; wish *for* rest; withdraw *from* bargain; wonder *at* his conduct; worthy *of* success; wrestle *with* difficulties.

Y

Yearn *for* home; yield *to* the outcry.

Z

Zest *for* pleasure.

Conjunctions

Conjunction is a word that joins words or sentences, for example : 'as', 'and', 'but', 'as well as', 'lest', 'or', 'as if', 'as soon as', 'yet', 'either or', 'rather', 'until', 'unless', 'who', 'when', 'since', 'hardly', 'too', 'not only/but also', 'now', 'well', 'both', 'also', 'neitner/nor', 'otherwise', 'else', nevertheless', 'whereas', 'while', 'however', 'therefore', 'so', 'then', 'so then', 'notwithstanding', 'supposing', 'though', 'although', 'according', 'scarcely', and many other such words.

Errors in the use of conjunctions

Incorrect	*Correct*
I met *no other* man *but* Mr. Datta.	I met *no other* man *than* Mr. Datta.
He has no other claim *except* his wealth.	He has no other claim *than* his wealth.

Note: After the adjective 'other' use 'than'. Don't use from, except, but.

As he has fever, *so* he cannot go with you.	*As* he has fever, he cannot go with you.

Note: 'As' is not followed by 'so' except for the sake of emphasis : 'As you sow, so shall you reap.'

Both Mohan and his brother were not there.	*Neither* Mohan *nor* his brother was there.

Note: 'Both' has positive sense. In the negative sense, we should use 'neither/nor' in the place of 'both'.

Both Avinash *as well as* Subhash were present there.	*Both* Avinash and Subhash were present there.
Lions are *both found* in Asia and Africa.	Lions are *found both* in Asia and Africa.

Note: If the conjunction 'both' is used, it should be followed by 'and' and not by 'as well as'. Also 'both' should be placed immediately before the words to which it refers.

He is very noble, *but* helps the poor.	He is very noble *and* helps the poor.
College life is charming *and* school life is dull.	College life is charming *but* school life is dull.

Note: 'And' is to join two words or clauses of the same nature. "But" is to join two antithetical clauses.

He is *not* only handsome *but* sensible.	He is *not only* handsome *but also* sensible.
He *not only* lost his ticket *but also* his luggage.	He lost *not only* his ticket, his luggage *also*.

Note: The proper correlative of 'not only' is 'but' or 'but also'. They should be followed by words of the same parts of speech.

He dresses *like* his brother.	He dresses *as his brother does*.

Note: 'Like' should not be used as a conjunction in the sense of 'as', although such a use may be allowed in conversation.

He does not speak *before* he is compelled.	He does not speak *unless* he is compelled.
Neither did I go *nor he went.*	Neither did I go *nor did he.*
Neither did I read *nor I wrote.*	Neither did I read *nor did I write*

Note: 'Neither' is always complemented by 'nor'. If 'neither' is followed by an auxiliary verb, 'nor' should be followed by the same auxiliary verb.

I doubt *that* he will come.	I doubt *whether* he will come.

Note: 'Come' should be taken not to use 'that' in place of 'if', 'when', 'whether', and 'though'.

The choice is between glorious death *or* shameful life.	The choice is between glorious death *and* shameful life.
His hat is *equally* beautiful as that of mine.	His hat is *as* beautiful as that of mine.
His success is *not remarkable as* the success of my brother.	His success is *not so* (or *as remarkable as* the success of my brother.

Note: 'Equally' and 'as' are not true correlatives. When 'as' is used as conjunction to denote equality of degree, it should be preceded by 'as' in the affirmative clause or by 'so' or 'as' in a negative one.

Before you *will come* Ranjit will have left.	Before *you come* Ranjit will have left.

Note: When the conjunctions 'when', 'while',

'before', 'tell', and 'after' are used in the subordinate sentences with reference to some future event, they are not followed by a verb in the future tense even when the verb in the principal clause is in the future.

Because he is dull, *therefore* he is punished.	He is dull, *therefore* he is punished or-Because he is dull, he is punished.

Note: 'Because' and 'therefore' should not be used in the same sentence.

He took a different attitude *than* what he used to take.	He took a different attitude *from* what he used to take.

Note: After 'different' do not use 'than', use 'from'.

When you insult me I must go away.	*Since* you insult me I must go away.

Note: 'When' refers to point of time. It should not be used for 'since'.

I fear he might die.	I fear *that* he might die.
I hope Sham will recover.	I hope *that* Sham will recover.

Note: Use 'that' after 'fear' and 'hope'.

Take care of him *until* he is with you.	Take care of him *as long as* he is with you.
Now you have come, you relieve me.	Now *that* you have come, you relieve me.
Directly he comes, I shall go.	*As soon as* he comes, I shall go.

He is *not* hardworking *or* intelligent.	He is *neither* hardworking *nor* intelligent.
When I saw a lion, *then* I was afraid.	When I saw a lion, I was afraid.
We shall try and find them.	We shall try *to* find them.
He was afraid *as soon as* I came back.	He was afraid *until* I came back.
Not only he is a poet but an artist.	*Not only* is he a poet *but* he is an artist *also*.
The college is beautiful where he studies.	The college where he studies is beautiful.
This is the *reason* I do not help you.	This is the *reason why* I do not help you.
He is *equally good as* his brother.	He is *as good as* his brother.
He was angry, *therefore* I ran away.	He was angry, *so* I ran away.
Immediately I saw him I recognised him.	*As soon as* I saw him I recognised him.
He had no choice *than* to yield.	He had no choice *but* to yield.
Hardly I had reached home *that* the rain started.	Hardly I reached home *when* the rain started.
He had scarcely reached the station *than* the train started.	He had scarcely reached the station *when* the train started.

Note: 'Hardly' is followed by 'when' and 'scarcely' by 'before' or 'when', but not by 'but', 'than' or 'that'.

Though he worked hard *but* he failed.	Though he worked hard *yet* he failed.

Note: 'Though' is followed by 'yet', and not by 'but'.

No sooner we reached there *when* it began to rain.	No sooner did we reach there *than* it began to rain.

Note: 'No sooner' is followed by 'than', not by 'then' or 'when' or 'but'.

He is the same boy *whom* I met last week.	He is the same boy *that* I met last week.
This is good, if not better than that.	This is *as good as* if not better than that.
I regard him my brother.	I regard him *as* my brother.

Note: Certain words as 'regard', 'depict', 'mention', 'treat', 'define', 'present', 'describe', 'portray', are always followed by 'as'.

Surinder will be appointed *as* a head clerk.	Surinder will be appointed a head clerk.

Note: Certain words (verbs) as 'call', 'appoint', 'elect', 'make', 'name', 'choose', 'consider', 'think' are not followed by 'as' or 'to be'.

He weeps as if he is poor.	He weeps as if he *were* poor.
You act as though you *are* sad.	You act as though you *were* sad.

Note: Do not use present tense after 'as if' and 'as though'; use 'were' in the present tense and 'had been' in the past tense.

Walk slowly lest you *may not* fall.	Walk slowly lest you *should* fall.
He ran away lest you *should not* be punished.	He ran away, lest you *should* be punished.

. **Note**: 'Lest' is negative and should not be followed by 'not'. After 'lest' use 'should'.

Unless you do not go there you cannot see him.	*Unless you go* there you cannot see him.
Wait here *until I do not come.*	Wait here *until I come.*

Note: 'Unless', 'untill' 'if not', 'so that' should not be used in a negative sentence.

I have taken this shop two weeks since.	I took this shop two weeks since.
I did not see you since you wrote last.	I have not seen since you wrote last.
Two weeks have passed.	Two weeks have passed.
He asked me that where his book was.	He asked me where his book was.
He asked me *that how you are.*	He asked me *how I was.*

Note: 'That' should not be used before a sentence in the direct narration, or after a verb denoting a question in the indirect speech.

Word order

Either the action was just or unjust.	The action was *either* just or unjust.

He or she is at fault.	*Either* he or she is at fault.
Did you go to his hostel or house.	Did you go to his hostel or *to* his house.
He was chosen *to be* a captain.	He was chosen a captain.
I have never written *nor* spoken to him.	I have never written *or* spoken to him.
She did not break it *nor* lose it.	She did not break it *or* lose it.
Your book is as good or better than mine.	Your book is as good *as* or better than mine.
The choice is between freedom *or* slavery.	The choice is between freedom *and* slavery.
This is the book I was telling you *about it*.	This is the book *about which* I was telling you.
Both Hari *as well as* Mohan was absent.	*Both* Hari and Mohan were absent.
Do not go out until they come back.	Do not go out till they come back.
So far they are concerned.	*So far as* they are concerned.
I have *got* nothing to say.	I have nothing to say.
This is the *same* pen *which* he gave me.	This is the *same* pen *as* he gave me.
Wait *while* I come, I won't be long.	Wait *till* I come, I won't be long.
Neither he is intelligent nor industrious.	He is *neither* intelligent nor industrious.
I don't know him *like* you do.	I don't know him *as* you do.
We did nothing else *than* cry.	We did nothing else *but* cry.

He asked *that whether* I knew what I was saying.	He asked *whether* I knew what I was saying.
They enquired *that where* was my office.	They enquired *where* my office was.
He must wait for me *until* it rains.	He must wait for me *while* it rains.
I prefer to die *than* yield.	I prefer to die *rather than* yield.
He could not finish all his work. *Therefore*, his case cannot be considered.	He could not finish all his work. His case, *therefore*, cannot be considered.

Note: 'Therefore' is used after a word or phrase that is emphasised.

Tell me when *are you* coming here?	Tell me when *you are* coming here?
Please tell me *when is* the train due to arrive here.	Please tell me *when* the train *is* due to arrive here.

Note: In a subordinate clause, question form is changed to assertive form.

Word Order

The house was demolished by the town committee *that was in the bazar.*	The house *that was in the bazar* was demolished by the town committee.
They attached *Mohan's house whom* they arrested.	They attached *the house of Mohan whom* they arrested.

For sale: a piano, the property of a captain with carved legs.	For sale: a piano, with carved legs, the property of a captain.

Note: Words thought of together must be kept together.

(*i*) A relative pronoun or verb should be placed as close to its antecedent as possible.

(*ii*) When a noun or a noun phrase or a clause is in opposition to a noun, it should not be separated from it by any word.

(*iii*) An adverb qualifying a sentence as a whole is placed at the beginning.

Until you work hard, you will improve.	*As long as* you work hard, you will improve.
He worked hard lest he *should not* fail.	He worked hard lest he *should* fail.
He must *either* leave or I.	*Either* he or I must leave.
No sooner he left the place, it began to rain.	No sooner did he leave the place *than* it began to rain.
Supposing if you fail, what will you do.	*Supposing* (or *if*) you fail, what will you do.
Unless you *do not* work hard, you cannot pass.	*Unless* you work hard, you cannot pass.
Not only did he abuse me, *but* beat me *also*.	He *not only* abused me *but also* beat me.

A Few Useful Hints

Hardly is always followed by 'when' not 'than'.

Scarcely is always followed by 'before' or 'when'.

No sooner is followed by 'than', not 'then'.

Such is always followed by '*as*'.

Lest is invariably followed by 'should'.

Either is followed by 'yet', not 'but'.

Not only is followed by 'but also'.

Former is followed by 'latter', not later.

Though is followed by 'yet', not 'but'.

Senior, junior, inferior, superior, prior, prefer, preferable, is followed by 'to', not 'than'.

One is followed by one's, not 'his' or 'her'.

Both is complemented by '*and*' not by 'as well as'.

Rather is followed by 'than', not 'then'.

Whether is paired with 'or'. *As* is paired with '*as*'.

So is paired with 'as'.

Other is paired with 'than'.

Some is used to show quantity in the affirmative sentences.

Any is used in the negative sentences. Example : 'He has got *some* money'. He did not give me *any* book'.

Infinitives, Participles and Gerund

ERRORS COMMITED IN THE USE OF THEM

A participle is a verb form which does the work of an adjective, e.g. 'I saw the *rising* sun'.

A Gerund is a verbal form which does the work of a noun, e.g. '*Swimming* is a good exercise'.

Incorrect	*Correct*
You need *not to worry.*	You need *not worry.*
He had *better to give* up his studies.	He had *better give up* his studies.
I hope to *have met* you.	I hope to *meet* you.
Playing hockey, *my leg was broken.*	Playing hockey, *I broke my leg.*
I prevented him *to go* there.	I prevented him *from going* there.
I forbade him *from smoking.*	I forbade him *to smoke.*
He succeeded *to win* the election.	He succeeded *in winning* the election.
Give me a *blotting.*	Give me a *blotting paper.*
She lives in the *boarding.*	She lives in the *boarding house.*
Sitting in my room, *the radio could be heard.*	Sitting in my room, *I could hear the radio.*
Being very cold, I kept indoors.	*It being very cold,* I kept indoors.

I did not know about *him coming*.	I did not know about *his coming*.
You may depend on *me coming* in time.	You may depend on *my coming* in time.
I insisted on *him* going there.	I insisted on *his* going there.

Shall and Will

IN ASSERTIVE SENTENCES

1(*a*) 'Shall' in the first and 'will' in the second and third persons express simple future tense; *e.g.* :

I shall go to school tomorrow.
You will go home tomorrow.
He will tell a story.

Note: Here 'shall' and 'will' are used as auxiliary verbs because they help other verbs to form the future tense.

(*b*) 'Shall' in the second and third persons points out either a command, a promise, a threat, a determination, or compensation, e.g. :

You shall attend the school tomorrow. (*command*)
He shall have his salary tomorrow. (*promise*)
He shall be dismissed if he disobeys. (*threat*)
They shall defend the fort. (*determination*)
You shall stay after the school. (*compulsion*)

Note: Have and shall is used as the *principal verb* and expresses meaning of its own, namely command or compulsion.

2 'Will' in the first person expresses willingness, intention, promise, threat or determination; *e.g.* :

I will see him tomorrow (*willingness*)

I will help you (*promise*)

I will not tolerate that (*threat*)

We will have our way (*determination*)

Note: Here 'will' is used as a *principal verb.*

3 'Will' in the third person sometimes expresses habit, e.g. : 'He *will* get up at five O'clock every morning and start work at six'.

In the interrogative sentences

1. 'Shall' in the first person and 'will' in the second and third denote simple enquiry; *e.g.*:
   Shall I bring a watch for you?
   Will you kindly lend me your bicycle?
   Will the school remain closed tomorrow?

Note: Sometime 'shall' in the third person denotes an enquiry for instructions or desire of the person addressed; *e.g.* : Shall he bring his son tomorrow? (Do you wish him to bring his son tomorrow.)

2. Sometimes 'will' is used with all persons to denote obstinacy (generally referring to past time); *e.g.*:
   The gun *will* not go off.
   He *will* not do his home task.

Mark the errors in the usage of *shall* and *will.*

Incorrect	*Correct*
He *will* drown and no one *shall* save him.	He *shall* drown and no one *will* save him.
Shall it rain today?	*Will* it rain today?

Shall she go to Dalhousie?	*Will* she go to Dalhousie?
"Tomorrow, there *will* be function," said the Director.	"Tomorrow, there *shall* be a function," said the Director.
I *will* be obliged to you for your hospitality.	I *shall* be obliged to you for your hospitality.
I am sorry I *will not* be able to go there.	I am sorry I *shall not* be able to go there.
I *will* help Ram, if he *will help* me.	I *will* help Ram, if he *helps* me.
I *shall* do or die,	I *will* do or die.
He *will* go there, it is a command.	He *shall* go there, it is a command.
The students *shall* know the result tomorrow.	The students *will* know the result tomorrow.
Shall Ram or *will* Prem do it?	*Will* Ram or *shall* Prem do it?
Will I open the window ?	*Shall* I open the window?

One should remember the following verse in connection with shall & will :

In the first person, simply **shall** *fortells*
In **will**, *a threat or else a promise dwells*
Shall *in the second and third both threat,*
Will *simply then fortells the future fact.*

Some other important usages of 'should' and 'would'

'Would' and 'should' are the past forms of 'will' and 'shall'.

1. 'Should' is a principal verb when it expresses meaning of its own, namely, duty, obligation, or propriety. *e.g.* :

Children should obey their parents.

We should help the poor.

He should have attended the meeting.

'Should' is used for all persons.

'Should' as an auxiliary verb (*i*) expresses futurity for the standpoint of past time.

(*ii*) expresses supposition or used after the conjunction 'lest', *e.g.* :

I told him I *should* leave the next day.

Should you go to him, give him my message.

He walked carefully, lest he *should* fall.

2. 'Would' expresses (*a*) meaning, such as determination, obstinacy or persistence; *e.g.* :

He would have his own way.

The house would not run however hard I tried.

(*b*) habitual action; *e.g.* :

He would go to the river every morning and swim.

The old man *would* come to stay for lunch.

(*c*) willingness, *e.g.* : 'He said he *would* help the boy.' 'Would' as Auxiliary verb expresses :

(*i*) futurity, *e.g.* : 'She said her father *would* return soon.'

(*ii*) conclusion of a condition contrary to fact; *e.g.* : If I were you, I *would* not leave the company.

(*iii*) polite form of question : 'Would you kindly bring a glass of water.'

May/Might

'May' as a principal verb expresses such meanings as:

(*i*) possibility *e.g.* : 'He may come today.'

(*ii*) permission, *e.g.* : 'You may go now.' 'May I go out ?'

(*iii*) as auxiliary it expresses purpose *e.g.* : 'He comes here so that he *may* see his sick son.'

(*iv*) a wish *e.g.* : '*May* he live long.'

'Might' is the past tense of 'may' and is sometimes used in the present tense, *e.g.* :

She worked hard so that she might win a scholarship.

She might leave just now.

She might leave next week.

'May' or 'might' do not express time with the same precision as other verbs; they express all the past, present and future tenses.

Ought

'Ought' is used

(*i*) to express duty or moral obligation, *e.g.* : 'We ought to love our neighbours.'

(*ii*) to express advisability, *e.g.* : 'It ought to be done at once.'

(*iii*) to express some probability *e.g.* : 'He ought to win.'

(*iv*) to express a shortcoming, : *e.g.* 'You ought to help your brother.'

Must

'Must' denotes

(*i*) fixed determinaton, *e.g.* : 'I *must* finish this before night.'

(*ii*) certainty, *e.g.* : 'It *must* rain today.'

(*iii*) compulsion, *e.g.* : 'You *must* come tomorrow.'

(*iv*) duty and obligation *e.g.* : 'We *must* obey our parents.'

Dare

The verb 'dare' is used in the sense of to venture or have courage, *e.g.* : 'He dare not insult me.'

Note: It takes an infinitive, without 'to', as its object.

'Dare' in the sense of 'to challenge' or 'to defy'

He dares to insult you.

He dared me to fight.

I dare you to cross this line.

Need

'Need' denotes necessity or obligation in the negative or interrogative sentence. It forms its third person singular in present tense without 's' and takes as its object an infinitive without 'to', e.g. :

He *need* not come here:

Need he mention this?

But when the verb 'need' is used in the sense of 'to require or 'to be in need of', the third person singular present tense is 'needs', *e.g.* : 'He *needs* some money,' 'This room *needs* some white washing'.

COMMON ERRORS—MISCELLANEOUS

Incorrect	*Correct*
Our teacher will *take* our test tomorrow.	Our teacher will *give* us a test tomorrow.
His brother will *give* examination next year.	His brother will *take* examination next year.

Note: A teacher or an examiner gives an examination or a test ; a candidate takes an examination or a test or sits for it.

What is the *fresh* news of today.	What is the *latest* news of today.

Note: News in edition is always latest. We however, can say 'fresh fruit', 'fresh milk', 'fresh butter', etc.

Good night, sir, we are happy you have come.	*Good evening*, sir, we are happy you have come.

Note: 'Good night' is used when we take leave of one another at night. At the time of meeting, we say, 'Good evening'.

Krishna gave me a *ten rupees* note.	Krishna gave me a *ten-rupee* note.

Note: The 'note' is one, so we say 'a ten-rupee

note'. However it is correct to say: 'He gave me ten rupees'.

Our hockey team *made* a goal in no time.	Our hockey team *scored* a goal in no time.
I saw a strange dream last night.	I had a strange dream at night/or I dreamt a strange dream.

Note: We 'have' a dream, not 'see' a dream ; and 'score' a goal, not 'make' one.

No *less* than 15 boys were present there.	No *fewer* than 15 boys were present there.
We want no *fewer* than five maunds of sugar.	We want no *less* five maunds of sugar.

Note: 'Less' denotes amount, degree or quantity or value; 'fewer' shows number. But we can say, 'I will not accept less than five rupees', because five rupees are regarded as a sum of money and not as a number of coins, we also say : "Lesser evil".

We must help *the poors*.	We must help *the poor*.

Note: Adjectives like 'poor' or 'blind' cannot take the plural form when they are used as noun in the plural.

Who will buy this house *for* such a price.	Who will buy this house *at* such a price.

Note: One should use 'for' only where a specific amount is mentioned, as ; "He sold his horse for five hundred rupees."

He has *left* riding.	He has *given up* riding.
Sham is my *cousin brother*.	Sham is my *cousin*.

Note: The word 'brother' is superfluous.

The two brothers are not on *talking terms* with each other.	The two brothers are not on *speaking terms* with each other.
Our president *gave* an impressive speech.	Our president *made* (or *delivered*) an impressive speech.

Note: 'Talking terms' is wrong. We 'make' or 'deliver' a speach and not 'give' a speech, but of course we 'give' a talk.

There is no *place* for you in the rickshaw.	There is no *room* for you in the rickshaw.

Note: 'Place' cannot be used in the sense of 'room' which means the unoccupied space.

The teacher did not allow me to *cut jokes* in the class.	The teacher did not allow me to *make jokes* in the class.

Note: We 'make', not 'cut', jokes.

My son is good *in* English.	My son is good *at* English.

Note: Similarly we should use 'clever at', 'poor at', 'quick at', 'slow at', etc.

Will you kindly *mend* this pencil?	Will you kindly *sharpen* this pencil?

Note: One 'sharpens' a pencil, but 'mends' a pen.

When will you *return back* from Agra?	When will you *return* (or *come back*) from Agra?

Note: The word 'back' after 'return' is superfluous, since 'return' means to come back.

Please write your answer *with* ink.	Please write your answer *in* ink.

Note: Always say write in chalk, write in pencil, but write with a pen.

Though he worked hard *but* he failed.	Though he worked hard *yet* he failed.
He fell *sick* just before the examination.	He fell *ill* just before the examination.

Note: 'To be sick' means to vomit or to be inclined to vomit or to be temporarily indisposed, for example; 'The smell in the room made me sick. 'But to be ill' means to be in bad health. However it is correct to say: 'The sick man is crying.'

Krishna came and sat *besides* me.	Krishna came and sat *beside* me.
Beside this pencil, I have two more.	*Besides* this pencil, I have two more.
He *resembles with* his brothers.	He *resembles* his brothers.
Will you *recommend for* me to your Director?	Will you *recommend me* to your Director?
This book *comprises of* six chapters.	This book *comprises* six chapters.
I have *ordered for* a cup of hot coffee.	I have *ordered* a cup of hot coffee.

I will *accompany with you* to Delhi.	I will *accompany you* to Delhi.
Why did you *reach at* the platform so late.	Why did you *reach* the platform so late.
He has not *joined in* any college so far.	He has not *joined* any college so far.
Why do you *shirk from* work?	Why do you *shirk* work?
He *attacked on me* all of a sudden.	He *attacked me* all of a sudden.
The lecturer *emphasised on* the need of discipline.	The lecturer *emphasised* the need for discipline.

Note: Certain verbs, like 'resemble', 'recommend', 'comprise', 'order', 'accompany', 'reach', 'join', 'shirk', 'attack', emphasise', 'discuss', 'fear', 'succeed', 'resist', 'request', 'pervade', 'precede', 'obey', 'violate', 'inform', 'assist', 'benefit', 'afford', etc., when used in the active voice are not followed by any preposition.

He *denied that* he was not a thief.	He *denied that* he was a thief.
The doctor *forbade* him *not* to drink.	The doctor *forbade* him to drink.
Hurry up *lest* we *may not* miss the train.	Hurry up *lest* we *should* miss the train.

Note: 'Unless', 'until', 'deny', 'forbid', 'lest', etc. are all negatives, so they should not be followed by another negative. In the case of 'lest' always use 'should' not 'may' or 'might'.

He *has died* last month.	He *died* last month.

Note: In the above sentence, 'last month' is past tense and 'has died' is present perfect whereas we should use both in the same tense. Therefore we should change 'has died' into 'died', past tense of 'die'.

I *think him as* a silly fellow.	I *think him* a silly fellow.

Note: Such verbs, as 'call', 'consider' 'think', appoint', 'effect', 'make', 'choose', etc., name terms are not followed by 'as'.

I *regard her my* sister.	I *regard her as* my sister.

Note: Some verbs, such as 'regard', 'describe', 'represent'. 'depict', 'portray', 'mention', 'define', 'treat', etc. are followed by 'as'.

What to speak of milk there was no water in the house.	*Not to speak of* milk there was no water in the house.

Note: 'what to speak of, is unidiomatic.

His *family members* have gone to Delhi.	His *family* has, or *the members of his family* have, gone to Delhi.

Note: The correct usage is a member or the family, not 'a family member'.

She gave me *advices.*	She gave me *a piece of advice* (or/*much advice*, or/*many pieces of advice*).

Note: 'Advices' means information of reports; it is not the plural of 'advice'.

Put off your dirty clothes.	*Take off* your dirty clothes.
He *took out* his hat.	He *took off* his hat.

Note: The opposite of 'put on' is 'take off'; not 'put off'; 'put off' means postpone.

Sushila got *passing marks* in English.	Sushila got *pass marks* in English.

Note: 'Passing marks' is Indianism; it is a wrong usage.

He *prefers* this house *than* that.	He *prefers* this house *to* that.

Note: 'Prefer', 'preferable,' 'inferior', 'junior', 'superior', 'senior', 'prior', etc. are always followed by 'to', not 'than'. We should not use 'more' before these adjectives.

We shall not go there if it will *rain.*	We shall not go there if it *rains*.

Note: We should not use two future tenses together ; one of them beginning with 'when' or 'if' should be in the present indefinite, and the other one in the future tense.

He admitted that he *has broken* the inkpot.	He admitted that he *had broken* the inkpot.
Our teacher told us that honesty *was* the best policy these days.	Our teacher told us that honesty *is* the best policy these days.

Note: If the Principle clause is in the past tense,

the subordinate clause must be in the past tense, unless it contains a universal or habitual truth.

Tell me *that* how *is he*?	Tell me *how is he*?

Note: When there are two sentences we should not use that, before, where, when, how, what, which and who, the subordinate clause should not be in the question form.

We shall start after *the* dinner.	We shall start *after dinner*.

Note: The definite article should not be used before the names of the meals, breakfast, lunch, dinner or supper.

We had a nice *play* of tennis.	We had a nice *game* of tennis.

Note: We should not use 'play' in the sense of 'game'. 'Play' means amusement, e.g. 'I am very fond of play'. or 'The play will be staged by the dramatic club.'

He *seldom or ever* smokes.	He *seldom or never* smokes.

Note: 'Seldom' is negatiave in sense, so it must alternate with 'never'.

It is too hot *that* we cannot go out.	It is too hot *to* go out or It is *so* hot *that* we cannot got out.

Note: 'Too' is used in the negative. We must use 'to' with 'too'. When we use 'so', we must use 'that'.

Ram *did* no mistake in dictation.	Ram *made* no mistake in dictation.

Note: We make a mistake and not 'do' it.

What *kind of a* friend are you?	What *type of* friend are you?

Note: Do not use 'a' or 'an' (the indefinite article after the phrase 'type of', 'sort of' or 'kind of' are collogenial, and so, should be avoided).

He bore *cheerfully* his miseries.	He bore *his miseries* cheerfully or He cheerfully bore *his miseries.*

Note: In the case of a transitive verb, use the adverb after the object.

We go to college with a view to *study.*	We go to college with a view to *studying.*

Note: 'With a view to' is always followed by a gerund and not an infinitive.

Will you kindly *open* this knot?	Will you kindly *untie* this knot?
We *slept* rather late last night.	We went *to bed* rather late last night.
Krishna left for Delhi by 12.40 *O'clock* train.	Krishna left for Delhi by *12.40* train.
Kamal will leave Ludhiana *train.*	Kamal will leave Ludhiana by *the 5 O'clock train.*

Note: When minutes or fraction of hour are given. like 5.50. half past three, 'o'clock' is not used. But for a full hour number we can use 'o'clock', e.g. We will start by the 5 o'clock train.

The Taj is a *worth seeing building.*	The Taj is a *building worth seeing.*
The Gita is worth reading.	The Gita is a *book* worth reading.

Note: A compound adjective formed by the combination of 'worth' with some participle (the verb used as an adjective) is placed after the noun it qualifies.

Out of a hundred as *much* as 60 boys have passed.	Out of a hundred as *many* as 60 boys have passed.
He wants as *many* as 10 kilos of wheat.	He wants as *much* as 10 kilos of wheat.

Note: 'As much as' denotes quantity where 'as many as' denotes number.

I bought 10 pears, out of *whom* five were rotten.	I bought 10 pears out of *which* five were rotten.

Note: 'Who' and 'whom' are used for living things, 'which' for lifeless things.

Why *you were* late yesterday?	Why *were you* late yesterday?

Note: In questions beginning with an interrogative word like 'what', 'when', 'why', 'where', 'how', 'which' the verb is placed before the subject, as in all questions.

He asked me what novel did I *study*.	He asked me what novel I *studied*.

Note: In indirect questions the usual order of words is followed, i.e., subject first, then Verb.

Our examination is *approaching near.*	Our examination is *approaching* or *drawing near.*
His uncle is *50 years.*	His uncle is *50 years old* (or is *50*).

Note: Either drop the word 'years' or use the complete expression : is 50 years old.

Stealing is a bad *custom.*	Stealing is a bad *habit.*
Indians have strange *habits.*	Indians have strange *customs.*

Note: A 'habit' belongs to an individual but a 'custom' belongs to a society or a country.

Many a boy *have* passed this year.	Many a boy *has* passed, (or many *boys have* passed) this year.

Note: 'Many a' is singular, so the Noun and the Verb must be singular.

One must love *his* religion.	One must love *one's* religion.
The ship *was drowned* and the passengers *were sunk.*	The ship *sank* and the passengers *were drowned.*

Note: Lifeless things are 'sunk' and living things are 'drowned', 'One' is followed by 'one'.

He is an *America returned.*	He *has been to* America.

Note: This is an Indianism.

Incorrect	Correct
To laugh or *cry* is entirely our own choice.	To laugh or *to cry* is entirely our own choice.

Note: When 'and' or 'or' link two dissimilar notions, 'to' must be inserted with each infinitive.

Incorrect	Correct
I *never* saw him today.	I *did not see* him today.

Note : 'Never' means 'not ever' except when used for very strong emphasis.

Incorrect	Correct
He *Neither speaks* English nor Hindi.	He *speaks neither* English nor Hindi.

Note: Correlative conjunctions that is, conjunctions used in pairs, like 'neither nor' 'not only but also' should be placed before words of the same part of speech.

Incorrect	Correct
The *train left* before I reached the station.	The train *had left* before I reached the station.

Note: In such sentences, the earlier action should always take the past perfect verb.

Incorrect	Correct
He talks as if he *is* my boss.	He talks as if he *were* my boss.

Note: Such expressions like 'as if', 'as though', etc., are always followed by the past tense plural.

Incorrect	Correct
He is 50 years old, isn't *it*?	He is 50 years old *isn't he*? (or *isn't that so*?)

Note: The object of the verb in the second part of the sentence 'is he not it.'

I cannot bear *her separation.*	I cannot bear *separation from her.*
I have finished *3/4* of this book.	I have finished *three-fourths* of this book.

Note: 'Three-fourths' implies three parts out of four. therefore, use the plural form.

He gets a monthly allowance of hundred rupees only.	He gets a monthly allowance of *a* hundred rupees only.

Note: The word 'hundred' must always be preceded by the indefinite article 'a'. A hundred paise makes one rupee.

He has read the *two first chapters* of this book.	He has read the *first two chapters* of this book.

Note: There cannot be two first chapters, just as there cannot be two last chapters.

What is the *cost* of this book?	What is the *price* of this book?

Note: 'Price is the amount of money paid by the customers. 'Cost' is the amount of money paid by the shopkeeper at the time of his purchase. We may ask the shopkeeper, how much did this book cost you?

His watch goes *five minutes behind.*	His watch is slow *by five minutes.*

Note: A watch is 'fast' or 'slow', not 'goes behind' or 'in front'. We can say: "My watch gains or loses . . ."

The train leaves at *eight and a half.*	The train leaves at *half past eight.*

Note: In telling time, we say 'half past two' or 'half past four', etc.

I met a *fat gentleman* today.	I met a *fat man* today.

Note: We use 'gentleman' only when we refer to a man's character, e.g. He is a thorough gentleman.

Krishan has grown into a beautiful youth.	Krishan has grown into *a handsome* youth.

Note: We generally use the word 'handsome' or 'good-looking' in case of a man and 'beautiful or pretty' in the case of a woman.

Mohan always *tells the truth* but Krishna always *speaks lie.*	Mohan always *speaks the truth* but Krishna always *tells a lie.*

Note: We 'speak' the truth, but 'tell' a lie.

Being a holiday today we went out for a walk.	*It being* a holiday today we went out for a walk.
Walking on the road, a snake bit him yesterday.	*As he was walking* on the road, a snake bit him yesterday.
Instead of his hard work, he failed.	*In spite* of his hard work, he failed.
In spite of going to the college he went to the cinema.	*Instead* of going to the college he went to the cinema.

Incorrect	Correct
I called *at* him yesterday.	I called *upon* him yesterday.

Note: We 'call upon' a person, but 'call at' a place.

Incorrect	Correct
Hari is the *mutual friend* of Sohan and Mahan.	Hari is the *common friend* of Sohan and Mohan.
He is my *fast enemy*.	He is my *bitter enemy*.

Note: We always have a fast friend or 'deadly' enemy.

Incorrect	Correct
Two months have passed since I *see* him.	Two months have passed since I *saw* him.

Note : If 'since' is used as a conjunction, the verb of the subordinate clause must be in the past indefinite.

Incorrect	Correct
Sham sang *beautiful*.	Sham sang *beautifully*.

Note: An adverb should be used to qualify a verb not an adjective.

Incorrect	Correct
Sugar tastes *sweetly*.	Sugar tastes *sweet*.

Note: After such verbs as 'look', 'feel', 'sound', 'taste', 'smell', an adjective instead of an adverb is used.

Incorrect	Correct
Nobody will miss him *like* I shall.	Nobody will miss him *as* I shall.

Note: 'Like' shows comparison.

Incorrect	Correct
The *economical* condition of Bangladesh is not good.	The *economic* condition of Bangladesh is not good.

Note: 'Economical' means thrifty: *We should be economical in our life.*

We study the *story* of the Muslims.	We study the *history* of the Muslims.

Note: A 'story' is an account of events which may or may not be true while 'history' is a systematic record of past events.

He has no *other* object *but* to earn money.	He has no *other* object *than* to earn money.
He behaved *friendly.*	He behaved *in a friendly way.*
He was *hardly hit* by his mother's death.	He was *hard hit* by his mother's death.

Note: 'Hardly' means just a little, so hard should be used.

Never *I have* seen such a person.	Never *have I* seen such a person.

Note: When 'never', 'seldom', 'rarely', 'neither', 'nor', 'not only', 'so sooner' are placed at the beginning of a complete clause, the verb must come before the subject as in a question.

He speaks *the English* fluently.	He speaks *English* fluently.
English left India in 1947.	*The English* left India in 1947.

Note: The definite article 'the' is never used before the names of languages. But we can say, 'He speaks the English language fluently.' 'The English' means the English people etc.

I cannot find my pencil *nowhere.*	I cannot find my pencil *anywhere.*

Note: We should not use double negative.

I hope she will *fail.*	I hope she will *pass.*

Note: We 'hope' for a good thing, but 'fear' for a bad thing.

He must *carry* my orders.	He must *carry out* my orders.
Just *hear* me please.	Just *listen to* me please.

Note: When attention is required, we use 'listen to'.

I *took ill* and could not go there.	I *was taken ill* and could not go there.

Note : Expression is used in the passive form.

The *roads* of Amritsar are narrow.	The *streets* of Amritsar are narrow.

Note: A 'street' is a way in a form with buildings on the sides but 'road' denotes a way leading from one place to another.

This pen will do *equally as well.*	This pen will do *equally well.*

Note: In the phrases 'equally as', 'equally as well' 'equally as great', etc., we should omit 'as'.

He *prohibited me to pluck* flowers.	He *prohibited me from plucking* flowers.
Abstain to speak ill of others.	*Abstain from* speaking ill of others.

Note: Certain words do not take infinitive but they require a preposition followed by a gerund. Some of these words are : 'Prevent', 'fond', 'keen', 'persist' 'refrain', 'insist', 'prohibit', 'abstain', 'confident', 'insist', 'assist', 'hinder', 'check'.

Last but *not the least* is the matter of discipline now before this meeting.	Last but *not least* is the matter of discipline now before this meeting.

Note: Last in number not in importance. So we should omit 'the' before 'least'.

His failure is *owing* to his illness.	His failure is *due to* his illness.
Due to poverty he cannot buy the books.	*Owing to* (or on account of) poverty, he cannot buy the books.

Note: 'Due to' must qualify some noun or pronoun; but 'owing to' is needed to govern the noun that follows. 'Due to' is generally used when due is predecative after the verb 'to be'.

What is the *reason* of a dust storm?	What is the *cause* of a dust strom?
He has a good *cause* for coming here.	He has a good *reason* for coming here.

Note: 'Cause' is that which produces a result, a 'reason' is that which explains or justifies a result.

We are going to *substitute* the old books by the new ones.	We are going *to replace* the old books by the new ones/We are going to *substitute* new books for the old ones.

Note: We substitute 'new' thing for 'old' one, but we replace the 'old' things by 'new' ones.

Krishan is *as good* or even *better* than his cousin.	Krishan is *as good as* or even better than his cousin.

Note: 'As' used to denote comparability is followed by another 'as', e.g. 'as nice as', 'as wonderful as' etc.

Let you and *I* do this work.	*Let* you and *me* do this work.

Note: 'let' is followed by a noun or pronoun in the objective case, like, 'him', 'her', 'me' etc.

Our elders *resemble* a tree which protects and gives cool shade.	Our elders can be *compared* (or liked) to a tree which protects and gives cool shade.

Note: 'Resemble' is used for things which look similar, e.g, 'The son resembles his father.

I request you *to kindly grant* me leave from the office.	I request you *kindly to grant* me leave from the office.

Note: An adverb should not be placed between an infinitive and its sign 'to'.

Neither he nor his brothers *is* to blame.	Neither he nor his brothers *are* to blame.

Note: In 'neither nor', 'either or', the verb should follow the second noun or pronoun.

My friends as well as I *am* busy.	My friends as well as I *are* busy.

Note : When two subjects not of the same person are joined by 'as well as', the verb agrees with the first subject.

It is a secret *between* you and *I*.	It is a secret *between* you and *me*.

Note: 'Between' is a preposition and all prepositions take the objective case after them.

Please give me *little* milk.	Please give me *a little* milk.
I have *few* friends whom I respect.	I have a *few* friends whom I respect.

Note: 'Little' means not much, practically nothing. 'A little' means some at least. Similarly 'few' means practically none. 'A few' means some at least.

I have not *replied* him so far.	I have not *answered* him so far.

Note: We 'answer' a person, but 'reply' to a note.

He bought pen, ink and paper, the *latter* being foolscap sheets.	He bought pen, ink and paper, the *last* being foolscap sheets.

Note: 'Latter' is always used in referring to the second of the only two things previously mentioned, not the 'last' of more than these two things.

Boys work hard *because* they may pass.	Boys work hard *so that* they may pass.

Note: 'Because' expresses some cause or reason, 'I will not attend the lecture because I am ill'; 'so that' is used to express a purpose.

Stop *to write.*	Stop *writing.*

Note: A gerund should not be confused with an infinitive.

Our wedding *comes of tomorrow.*	Our wedding *comes off* tomorrow.
She *comes off* a noble family.	She *comes of* a noble family.

Note: To 'come off' means to take place, to be held.

Hari's brother does not *care for* his money.	Hari's brother does not *take care of* his money.
Hari *does not care* for my advice.	Hari *pays no attention* to my advice.
Care for him when I am gone.	*Take care of* him when I am gone.

Note: 'Care for' cannot be used in the sense of 'take care of'. To 'care for' means to like, as, 'I do not care for him', but to 'take care of' means to look after.

I doubt *if* she will pass.	I doubt *that* she will pass.

Note: With 'doubt' or 'doubtful', we should use 'that' and not 'if' or 'whether' when mentioning that which is doubted.

Do not *make castles* in the air.	Do not *build castles* in the air.
You are *abusing* your father's money.	You are *misusing* your father's money.

Note: We misuse money and abuse power.

Of these two lamps this is the *besı*.	Of these two lamps this is the *better*.

Note: To compare two persons or things we should use the comparative degree, but in case of more than two persons or things, we should use superlative degree.

Hari is the *ablest of all other* students.	Hari is the *ablest of all* students.
Sham is *cleverest of* all other friends.	Sham is *cleverer than* any other friend.

Note: We shoula use 'any' 'other', 'than', only in comparative degree, not at all in the superlative degree.

Whom do you think will become our new President.	*Who* do you think will become our new President.
We do not know *who* he punished.	We do not know *whom* he punished.

Note: 'Who' is used for subject and whom for object.

Bread and milk *are* his only food these days.	Bread and milk *is* his only food these days.

Note: If two subjects together express an idea, the verb is in the singular.

Here are two pens, choose *any* of them.	Here are two pens choose *either* of them.
You can take *either* of these five books.	You can take *any* of these five books.
Neither of these four pens are yours.	*None* of these four pens is yours.

Note: When there are two things or persons, we should use 'either' or 'neither', but when there are more than two things or persons, we should use, 'any' or 'none'. The verb in both cases will be singular.

Each of the 20 girls *have* done their work.	Each of the 20 girls *has* done her work.
Everyone of them *have* done their work.	Everyone of them *has* done his work.
None of them in *their* senses would have done this.	None of them in *his* senses would have done this.

Note: 'Each', 'every', 'everyone', 'everybody', 'anybody', 'none', 'nobody', 'somebody' must always be followed by verbs, pronouns and adjectives in the singular.

We asked him *that* will he help me.	We asked him *if* (or *whether*) he would help me.

Note: When the answer is in 'yes' or 'no' we should use if or whether in the indirect narration.

I asked her *that when will she* go there.	I asked her *when she would* go there.

Note: We should not use that before 'which', 'where', 'when', 'why', 'how' 'who', 'what', etc, in the indirect form.

I am as honest as *him.*	I am as honest as *he.*

Note: The pronoun should be in the nominative and not in the accusative case.

Om is *one of my friend.*	Om is *one of my friends.*

Note: After 'one of' the noun is plural.

Today it is *bitter* cold.	Today it is *bitterly* cold.

Note: Here adverb 'bitterly' is needed.

I have *many works* to do today.	Today I have a *lot of work* to do.

Note: The plural form 'works' means a factory or the writings of an author, e.g. : I visited the iron works, or, "I have read the works of Milton."

Hari is devoted to gambling.	Hari is *addicted* to gambling.
He is *addicted* to praying.	He is *devoted* to praying.

Note: 'Addicted' is used in a bad sense and 'devoted', in a good sense.

The Germans *invaded the* French and attacked their country.	The Germans *attacked the* French and *invaded their* country.

Note: We 'attack' persons or people and 'invade' a country or town.

Supposing *if* he fails what would happen.	*Supposing* (or *if*) he fails what would happen.
Please *kindly* help me.	*Please* (or *kindly*) help me.

Note: 'Please' or 'kindly' mean the same thing. We use 'kindly' when we address a person superior to us.

The chair cost Rs. 50 in which he sat.	The chair in which he sat cost Rs. 50.
Ram moved *earth and heaven* to pass the examination.	Ram moved *heaven and earth* to pass the examination.
Wrong or right, I must do this work.	*Right or wrong,* I must do this work.

Note: Good things always come first, e.g. : Rich and poor; high or low; body and soul; heaven and earth, etc.

A miser can part *with* his son, but not *from* money.	A miser can part *from his* son but not with his money.

Note: We part 'from' a person and 'with' a thing.

Mohan *refused* the statement.	Mohan *denied* the statement.
Krishna *denied* the invitation.	Krishna *refused* (or *declined*) the invitation.

Note: 'Refuse' means to reject. 'Deny' means to refuse to acknowledge.

I met Mr. Sudhir Malhotra Esqr.	I met Mr. *Sudhir Malhotra* (or Sudhir Malhotra Esqr.)

Note: 'Mr' and 'Esqr' mean the same thing and both should not be used jointly. 'Mr.' is used in the beginning and Esqr. at the end.

A strong gust of *air* blew away my hat.	A strong gust of *wind* blew away my hat.
Your answer must not *exceed more than* ten pages.	Your answer should not *exceed* ten pages.

Note: 'Exceed' implies 'more than'. 'Air' is what we breathe and 'wind' is air in motion which makes the leaves of the trees move.

What is the *last* news of the match.	What is the *latest* news of the match.

Note: 'Latest' is the last up to the present. 'Last is the final one. e.g., 'I marched there last of all.

Our teacher *takes pain* for us.	Our teacher *takes pains* for us.

Note: 'Pains' means care of interests, as: A pains-taking teacher.

Say my compliments to your mother.	*Give* my compliments to your mother.
Read the *above* remarks.	Read the remarks *given above*.

Note: 'Above' is an adverb, note an adjective.

He is suffering from *eye-sore* today.	He is suffering from *sore eyes* today.

Note: 'Eyesore' means something you dislike or a thing of which you are envious e.g. : His wealth is an eye sore to him.

He *will* go there, it is a command.	He *shall* go there, it is a command.

Note: 'Shall' in the second and third persons denotes order, threat, compulsion, promise, determination, etc.

Sushil is a *hardworker* boy.	Sushil is a *hardworking* boy.
We must *revenge* our father.	We must *avenge* our father.
We must *revenge* our enemy.	We must *take revenge on* our enemy.

Note: To take 'revenge' is to wreak one's wrongs on the offender in a malignant spirit. To 'avenge' means to inflict punishment upon a person for a wrong done to ourselves or some other person.

Hari will come *just now*.	Hari will come *presently*.

Note: 'Just now' means present time or time just past. Presently' means immediately in the future.

I *have a mind to* go there.	I *intend going* there.

Note: To ' have a mind' is unidiomatic.

On Sunday he goes *to* cinema.	On Sunday he goes to the cinema.

Note: The definite article is needed before the words 'cinema', 'concert', 'theatre', etc.

Ram came to college *latter* than I.	Ram came to college *later* than I.

Note: 'Later' refers to time. 'I will see you later on'. 'Latter' implies order and means the second of the two things just mentioned, as : 'Mohan and Sohan are friends.' The former (Mohan) is in business, the latter (Sohan) is in service.'

We will see you at *yours* this evening.	We will see you *at* your *house* this evening.

Note: 'Yours' is, of course, correctly used for house when the word house has been previously expressed. 'Shall we send it to his house or to yours'.

A piano is wanted by *a boy with carved legs.*	A *piano with carved legs* is wanted by a boy.

We, you and they will go there.	*You, they and we* will go there.

Note: We must use first the second person, then the third, and last of all the first person. Remember 2, 3, 1.

Ram is *cleverer than industrious.*	Ram is *more clever than he is industrious.*
Things are not *together as they seem.*	Things are not *altogether as they seem.*

Note: 'Altogether' is one word meaning the whole.

The hero's death is different. from the martyr.	The heor's death is different from the martyr's or from that of a martyr.
His book is *equally useful as* that of mine.	His book is *as useful as* that of mine.
The camera *costed* me two hundred rupees.	The camera *cost* me two hundred rupees.
The news was *broadcasted* today by A.I. Radio.	The news was *broadcast* today by A.I. Radio.

Note: The verb 'cost' 'broadcast', 'fit', etc. remain unchanged in the past and past participle forms.

Overwork will *effect* your health.	Overwork will *affect* your health.

Note: 'Affect' is verb and 'effect' is noun.

He lives *at England.*	He lives *in England.*
He is posted *in Verka at Amritsar* district.	He is posted *at Verka in Amritsar* district.

Note: 'In' is used with names of countries and big towns, like America, Delhi, Calcutta, etc. while 'at' is used when we speak of small towns or villeges.

Hari is proper *than anybody.*	Hari is proper *than anybody else.*

Note: In making comparisons the word else should be used after *everybody, anybody, anything.*

□ □ □

Also in Orient Paperbacks

How to Achieve Super Word Power

Ajay Rai

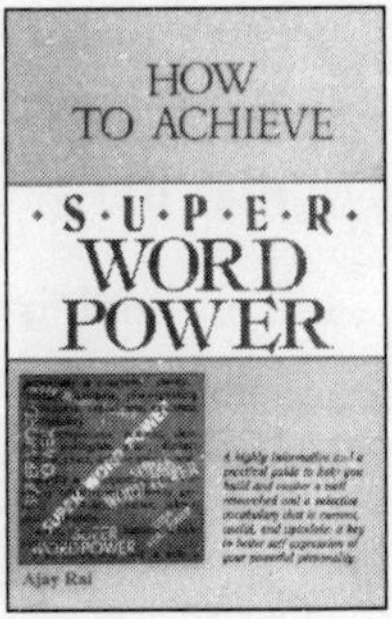

Discover the dynamic power of words! This book is designed and programmed to put you a step ahead of others; to help you acquire and command words that reflect clarity of thought, precision in communication and ensure your success in the world around you.

Participate actively in the tests/exercises given in this book. As you go through these exercises, you will come across new words, unfamiliar words and even foreign words now used with increasing frequency in the English language.

Think of these words! Write these words! Say the words aloud as you write them!

By the time you finish the book, you would have learnt and acquired over 500 new words, more than an average adult acquires in several years — words that will put you ahead of others.

Also in Orient Paperbacks

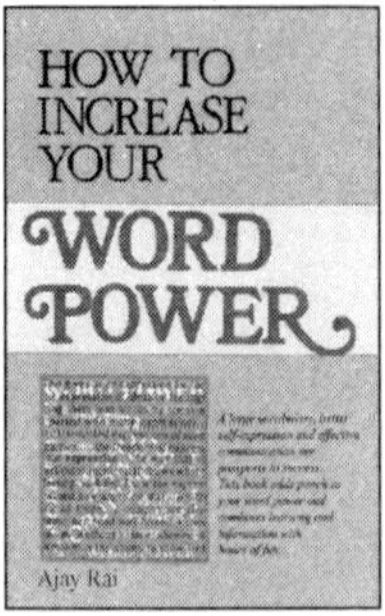

How to Increase Your Word Power

Ajay Rai

This book is designed to enhance your communication effectiveness. It will help you master vocabulary, to learn new words and new phrases. It is also designed to sort out your vocabulary problems and improve your language proficency.

The Word Power Tests given in the book are based on proven, step-by-step programme to equip you with words which will help you express clearly, convincingly, and forcefully. With each successive test you will not only enlarge your vocabulary, but also acquire necessary skill for precise and clear expression.

'The book seeks to help the reader develop his vocabulary by a number of devices...'

— *Pioneer*

Also in Orient Paperbacks

How to Speak & Write Better English

D.D. Vaid

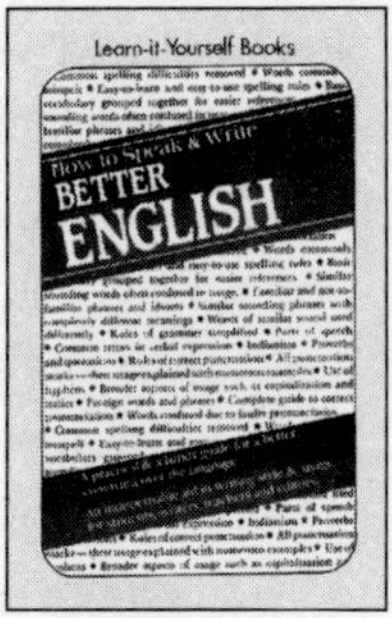

This book is specifically designed and written for those who are learning English as a second language. It aims to strengthen not only the writing ability but also command over spoken English. Chapters on spellings and punctuation provide easy-to-use and remember rules which would help the readers in developing and improving writing skills. Correct usage of similar sounding words, idioms, phrases and proverbs has been explained with hundreds of examples. A separate chapter on pronunciation based on IPA guidelines gives rules and examples of correct pronunciation. The main aim of the book is to make the reader learn modern and idiomatic style of spoken and written English.